MW00678032

Children's
Writing

*Perspectives From
Research*

Children's Writing

Perspectives From Research

Karin L. Dahl

The Ohio State University
Columbus, Ohio, USA

Nancy Farnan

San Diego State University
San Diego, California, USA

INTERNATIONAL
**Reading
Association**

800 Barksdale Road
PO Box 8139
Newark, Delaware 19714-8139, USA
www.reading.org

National Reading Conference
122 South Michigan Avenue
Suite 1100
Chicago, Illinois 60603, USA

IRA BOARD OF DIRECTORS

John J. Pikulski, University of Delaware, Newark, Delaware, *President* • Kathryn A. Ransom, Illinois State University, Springfield, Illinois, *President-Elect* • Carol Minnick Santa, School District #5, Kalispell, Montana, *Vice President* • Richard L. Allington, University at Albany–SUNY, Albany, New York • Betsy M. Baker, Columbia Public Schools, Columbia, Missouri • James F. Baumann, Department of Reading Education, University of Georgia, Athens, Georgia • James V. Hoffman, The University of Texas–Austin, Austin, Texas • Kathleen Stumpf Jongsma, Northside Independent School District, San Antonio, Texas • Adria F. Klein, California State University, San Bernardino, California • Diane L. Larson, Owatonna Public Schools, Owatonna, Minnesota • John W. Logan, Northbrook School District 27, Northbrook, Illinois • Lesley M. Morrow, Rutgers University, New Brunswick, New Jersey • Alan E. Farstrup, Executive Director

The International Reading Association attempts, through its publications, to provide a forum for a wide spectrum of opinions on reading. This policy permits divergent viewpoints without implying the endorsement of the Association.

NRC BOARD OF DIRECTORS
Martha Rapp Ruddell, Sonoma State University, Rohnert Park, California, *President* • Linda B. Gambrell, University of Maryland, College Park, Maryland, *President-Elect* • Taffy E. Raphael, Oakland University, Rochester, Michigan, *Vice President* • Peter Dewitz, University of Virginia, Charlottesville, Virginia, *Treasurer* • Lee Gunderson, University of British Columbia, Vancover, British Columbia, *Secretary* • Kathryn H. Au, University of Hawaii, Honolulu, Hawaii, *Past President* • Mark F.W. Condon, University of Louisville, Louisville, Kentucky • James Cunningham, UNC Charlotte, Charlotte, North Carolina • Peter Johnston, SUNY Albany, Albany, New York • Lea McGee, University of Alabama, Tuscaloosa, Alabama • Cathy M. Roller, University of Iowa, Iowa City, Iowa • Sheila Valencia, University of Washington, Seattle, Washington

Director of Publications   Joan M. Irwin
Assistant Director of Publications   Wendy Lapham Russ
Managing Editor, Books and Electronic Publications   Christian A. Kempers
Associate Editor   Matthew W. Baker
Assistant Editor   Janet S. Parrack
Assistant Editor   Mara P. Gorman
Publications Coordinator   Beth Doughty
Association Editor   David K. Roberts
Production Department Manager   Iona Sauscermen
Graphic Design Coordinator   Boni Nash
Electronic Publishing Supervisor   Wendy A. Mazur
Electronic Publishing Specialist   Anette Schütz-Ruff
Electronic Publishing Specialist   Cheryl J. Strum
Electronic Publishing Assistant   Peggy Mason

Copyright 1998 by the International Reading Association, Inc., and the National Reading Conference.

All rights reserved. No part of this publication may be reproduced or transmitted in any form or by any means, electronic or mechanical, including photocopy, or any informational storage and retrieval system, without permission from the publisher.

Library of Congress Cataloging in Publication Data
    Dahl, Karin L., 1938–
    Children's writing: Perspectives from research/Karin L. Dahl & Nancy Farnan.
       p.   cm.—(Literacy studies series)
    Includes bibliographical references and indexes.
    1. English language—Composition and exercises—Study and teaching (Elementary)   2. Report writing—Study and teaching (Elementary)   3. Children—Writing.   I. Farnan, Nancy. II. Title.   III. Series.
    LB1576.D12   1996   97-51433
    372.62'3—dc21
    ISBN 0-87207-189-8 (paperback)

Contents

CHAPTER 8

Thinking Back, Looking Ahead

Note From The Series Editors

The goal of the Literacy Studies Series is both to advance knowledge in the field of literacy and to help make research a more important focus in the literacy community. The volumes in the series therefore are intended to inform literacy instruction and research by reporting findings from state-of-the art literacy endeavors.

Karin L. Dahl and Nancy Farnan have compiled research that carefully examines and critiques what we do and do not know about children's writing. We selected *Children's Writing* for the series because never before has such an exhaustive study been undertaken to examine the writing processes and teaching-learning strategies of elementary school children and their teachers. In the past, most large-scale reviews have been limited to secondary school, college, or adult writers. Each chapter of this book pushes the reader toward the search for valid answers and the generation of new questions while also recommending ideas for classroom practice.

We hope that this volume plays the important role of informing teachers, researchers, and the larger educational community about the issue of teaching and learning to write in elementary schools. The authors of this volume report on the progress made in writing instruction. This volume will serve as a reference for current knowledge about writing in elementary schools and as a challenge inviting all educators to pursue research in the area that will be the foundation for future writing instruction.

We hope that the entire Literacy Studies Series will broaden understanding of research in specific areas. We also hope the series will provide guidance for designing the most effective instructional practices.

James Flood
Diane Lapp
Series Editors
San Diego State University
San Diego, California, USA

Foreword

Children's Writing: Perspectives From Research is one of the first two monographs in the new Literacy Studies Series produced jointly by the International Reading Association and the National Reading Conference. This publication marks an important collaboration between these two professional organizations, and it also signals two additional kinds of connections. One is a connection between reading and writing, as literacy educators have moved beyond old turf divisions of a "reading domain" that belongs to a reading profession and a "writing domain" that belongs to a writing profession. It makes sense today for two organizations, both devoted to literacy education and with "reading" in their names, to produce a book on writing. The other connection is a link between research and practice. This book is a synthesis of research, but it is a synthesis designed to have clear relevance to practice. It is this latter kind of connection that I want to highlight.

Karin L. Dahl and Nancy Farnan have identified teachers as their major audience. As I read the book, it seemed to me that Dahl and Farnan were providing answers to two major questions that teachers might ask: (1) What is the nature of children's writing processes? and (2) How do children's writing processes and products change as children's writing abilities develop? Moving from the first chapter on through the other seven chapters, readers learn about the nature of the composing process and about developmental patterns in writing ability. In so doing, they also learn more about how to teach in accordance with that knowledge.

The first major wave of research on the writing process, which began late in the 1970s, focused on cognitive aspects—mental processes, such as planning and revising. Although much of the research was conducted with adults, some dealt with children's writing and revealed certain strategies that are characteristic of children (for example, the "what next?" strategy). The book begins with a discussion of research focused on cognition.

In the latter years of the 1980s and throughout the 1990s, research has become situated in particular writing contexts, including the contexts of classrooms, and has emphasized social processes in composing. This is where Dahl and Farnan direct much of their attention throughout the book: the social aspects of writing. Writers write for audiences, they ask other people to read and comment on their drafts, and they incorporate ideas gained from prior reading into their own writing. As the authors point out, the research on such factors as audience awareness, response to writing, and writing from reading is quite relevant to instruction when teachers set up their classrooms and design lessons.

The research on developmental patterns is also important to teachers of writing, who should know what is typical of young writers at a particular age, what kinds of changes to expect, and what changes to foster through instruction. Some evidence of development, such as extensiveness of planning, have been documented by observing students. Other changes, such as elaboration and connectedness of content, have been discerned by analyzing the products of writing. Dahl and Farnan suggest various means, from portfolios to rubrics, that teachers can use for tracing development on the part of their own students.

Children's Writing may be a research monograph, but it is also a *practical* book in two senses of the word. It is practical in that much of its research-based material is derived from practice, particularly classroom practice. It is also practical in that knowledge gained from reading it can be applied to useful ends, in particular, better teaching of writing.

Nancy Nelson
Louisiana State University
Baton Rouge, Louisiana, USA

Introduction

What does research tell us about children's writing processes and about their writing development across the primary, intermediate, and middle-school grades? (In this book primary refers to K–2, intermediate refers to 3–5, and middle school refers to 6–8.) How can teachers design writing instruction that supports young writers at work and provides the structures and information that students need in order to improve? What do we know about skill development as children learn the craft of writing? What instructional practices has research documented as effective and which are less effective? What new directions are ahead for writing workshops and for writing across subject areas? How can writing be assessed in ways that inform the writer and the teacher?

We designed this book for teachers who are curious about what research on children's writing has to say about these questions and who are concerned about the writing processes and practices of students in the primary, intermediate, and middle-school grades. The book does not attempt to describe every study that has been conducted, but rather to provide a general sense of what has and has not been investigated in terms of children's writing and the writing instruction that takes place in classrooms. We highlight representative studies, describing some investigations in detail and others in general terms, with an emphasis on what their findings are and how those findings inform classroom writing instruction.

Included in the discussions of what research tells us about children's writing are studies found in leading research journals addressing literacy and also in books about writing instruction that are based on extended systematic work with children. We include reports by teacher researchers working in their own classrooms and suggest further investigations that need to be conducted in classrooms.

This book was written in the interest of furthering our understandings about children's writing processes. We highlight the important role of research in writing instruction for children, providing an organized framework around which we can discuss past and current research perspectives regarding the writing of children and young adolescents. Other research summaries and reviews exist. We can go back to Lyman's 1929 summary of research in which he concluded that the composing process was so complex that it could not be analyzed. In 1963, Braddock, Lloyd-Jones, and Schoer wrote *Research in Written Composition*, concluding that there were still many aspects of the composing process yet to be studied. In 1986, Hillocks compiled a comprehensive review of writing research between 1963 and 1982, *Research on Written Composition: New Directions for Teaching*, that contains approximately 2,000 bibliographic items. Others have likewise added to the body of knowledge about writing by synthesizing discrete research findings (Dyson & Freedman, 1991a; Jensen, 1993; Sperling, 1993).

The major distinction between the reviews mentioned in the preceding paragraph and our book is that they were written primarily for an audience of researchers, and this work is intended primarily for classroom teachers as well as the university researchers who work closely with them. Our goal, besides contributing to the thinking about writing and writing instruction, is to make the general research base accessible to classroom teachers and to illuminate some possible directions for further research as we concentrate on children and young adolescents' composing and on the work that teachers do in writing classrooms. As we developed this book, we were guided by a desire to capture the general trends from past research and describe selected studies that inform teachers' work in the classroom and, as a reflection of what research tells us, to illuminate that which needs to be investigated. In this process, we have established some boundaries, excluding purely anecdotal descriptions and testimonies about instructional approaches. We have focused instead on information from sound qualitative and quantitative research. Also excluded are studies addressing emergent writing that focus on learners younger than first grade and studies on handwriting.

An interesting note is that educational research in general, and in the area of writing in particular, has moved from primarily quantita-

2

tive reporting of data from quasi-experimental studies to include qualitative research conducted in the context of intact and functioning classrooms. The latter has led to a shift from strict research reporting to the development of research-based books for teachers that address instruction in writing. As examples, we think of Nancie Atwell, Carol Avery, Lucy Calkins, Donald Graves, Ralph Fletcher, Shelley Harwayne, and Linda Rief, and their work with elementary and middle school writers and their teachers. We think that such works have a significant impact on the teaching of writing, so we have included them along with our reporting of what may be considered more traditional research.

We are particularly interested in classroom research and have made an effort in this book to include the work of teacher researchers, as mentioned. As part of each chapter in a section called "Looking Ahead," we discuss issues and research questions that have the potential to spark classroom explorations. Several books, such as *Inside/Outside: Teacher Research and Knowledge* (Cochran-Smith & Lytle, 1993), *The Teacher-Researcher: How to Study Writing in the Classroom* (Myers, 1985), and *Opening the Door to Classroom Research* (Olson, 1990), explore the dual roles of teacher and researcher and describe the importance of classroom-based research conducted by teacher researchers. Myers argues that a call for teacher research is "not just a matter of professional politics," but rather "one of the most urgent needs for making schools better places for teaching and learning" (p. 2). Our intention is to engage teachers in inquiry and action research and to expand school-university research collaborations that center on children's writing and writing instruction.

Another intention of this work is translation, where possible, of research into practice. Although not all research cited in this book is appropriate for such an effort, many selected studies do have implications for teachers' work. Our sections in each chapter entitled "Classroom Implications" and "Ideas for Instruction" were designed to draw together these research implications and suggest instructional practices. These sections also serve as summaries of research trends across each specific topic.

Chapter 1 takes a historical look at conceptions of the writing process, including early writing-process investigations and models of what writers do when they write. It also examines the differences in the writing processes of novice and expert writers and describes the

3

conceptions of the writing process that come from practicing professional writers, including those who write for elementary and middle school children. Chapter 2 takes a look at what we know about the writing processes of children, examines their actions while composing, and describes writing-process research for children in the primary, intermediate, and middle-school grades. Chapter 3 centers on what we know about writing workshop programs and what future directions are suggested in research about writing instruction. In this chapter we also explore research on teacher-student conferences and the social dynamics of writing workshop programs.

Chapter 4 draws together research about the craft of writing; topics include children's awareness of audience, knowledge of planning, understanding of genres, and ability to revise. We also focus on research on spelling and punctuation as it develops within classroom writing programs. Chapter 5 extends writing instruction to writing across subject areas, including social studies, mathematics, and literature. It examines connections between writing and thinking and between writing and reading. In Chapter 6 we discuss the role of technology in the writing classroom and provide a collection of sites on the World Wide Web that offer avenues for further exploration. We also look at some of the issues raised by technology in the writing classroom and reflect on the changing role of the teacher in writing classrooms that include computers and access to the Internet. Chapter 7 provides a broad view of research on assessment and evaluation, including large-scale assessments, research on the use of portfolios and rubrics, investigations of teachers' written comments, and ways to ensure that assessment and instruction inform classroom practice and performance. And finally, Chapter 8 looks at the issues the book examines and their broad future implications.

Our intent is to support teacher exploration of this body of research and to stimulate further investigations from various research perspectives into children's writing. It is our goal that the classroom implications we present will be useful and that they will spark thoughts of other classroom practices that we may not have considered. We also hope, as we discuss ideas for future research, that readers will find some of the ideas compelling catalysts for their own inquiries into children's writing.

CHAPTER 1

Conceptions of the Writing Process

Over the past two decades, research interest in writing has shifted from studying the products of writing to studying the processes associated with how writers write (Dyson & Freedman, 1991b). This shift has occurred primarily because a singular emphasis on writing products did not serve teachers' understandings about how to support writers in their development, nor did it help teachers develop effective writing programs. Teachers' questions about how to teach writing have motivated and guided research interest in the writing process. Teachers and researchers have asked: How do writers write? What decisions do they make when they write? What problems do writers solve and how do they solve them? How do differing purposes and contexts influence children's writing? As researchers have used these questions to develop descriptions of writing processes, ideas about process-centered writing instruction evolved.

Writing-Process Definitions

It is nearly impossible to talk about writing instruction without the word *process*, as in the statement: *I teach process writing*. However, the modifier is redundant because writing *is* process. Writing can be defined as composing and expressing ideas through letters, words, art, or media and print, something that only occurs when mental operations (processes) are mobilized for the purpose of composing and expressing ideas. Other ways of defining writing all make reference to process as well. Murray (1985) describes writing as thought processes in action: "Meaning is not thought up and then written down. The act of writing is an act of thought" (p. 3).

Although we know that writing is process, explaining exactly how the process functions is far from easy. Dyson and Freedman (1991b) speak to the complexity of understanding writing process:

> Writing is conceived of as a skill and yet, at the same time, that skill is itself a process dependent upon a range of other skills and, moreover, a process that is kaleidoscopic, shaped by the author's changing purposes of writing. (p. 754)

The research of Bereiter and Scardamalia (1987) suggests that numerous demands in writing simultaneously compete for a writer's attention. The writing process is highly complex because of "the interdependency of components, which requires that a number of elements be coordinated or taken into account jointly" (p. 133).

The interdependent components of the writing process are not just limited to the cognitive or mental processes directly associated with producing text; they also include the nature of the writing task. Shifts in the task cause the writer to make large adjustments in the writing process or to create new writing processes (Murray, 1985). For example, a student writing a persuasive essay for an assignment may write several drafts, interspersed with feedback and revision opportunities. On the other hand, with 60 minutes to write an essay for an examination, this same student would work to produce a complete draft on the first writing, thereby having to change the process that worked for the persuasive essay. This relation between process and task is further complicated by the writer's sense of the social and cultural dynamics present in the classroom.

The complexity associated with the nature of writing and writing process underlies the complexity associated with the teaching of writing. Therefore, before we examine specific instructional techniques, we need to look closely at writing process.

In this chapter the focus is on the idea of writing process, how our thinking about writing process has changed, and how those changes have affected our thinking about writing and writing instruction. In our sketches of research, we describe shifts that have occurred in models of the writing process. We also consider writing research that addresses the effectiveness of writing-process instruction and sample the body of work that looks at professional writers and their ways of working.

Early Research on the Writing Process

The bulk of early research about writing process focused on writers of high school age and older, describing their composing processes through think-aloud protocols, which are verbal accounts of writers' actions and thoughts generated while writing. Emig (1971) is recognized as one of the first researchers to attempt such a study of composing processes. Her investigation of twelfth-grade students showed that students basically wrote in two modes: extensive writing and reflexive writing. Extensive writing is addressed to the teacher as audience—it is school writing with little attention to prewriting or to rethinking or contemplation of the written text. In contrast, the audience for reflexive writing (for example, poetry and personal writing) is most often a trusted peer or even the writer him- or herself. It involves contemplation of what is being written and more attention to revision.

Emig used her research to identify several categories of composing: planning, starting, composing aloud, reformulation (correcting, revising, and rewriting), stopping, and contemplation of the product. She found that "composing does not occur as a left-to-right, solid, uninterrupted activity with an even pace. Rather there are recursive, as well as anticipatory features" (p. 84). These processes were influenced by the context in which they occurred and were affected by the writer's sense of audience and purpose. As a result of her work with 12th graders, Emig noted that school seemed to have a significant, sometimes negative, influence on students' ability to think and behave like writers. Students' descriptions of their writing behaviors in school differed significantly from established writers' descriptions of their work. The writing-process research that followed Emig's study began to explore differences between skilled and unskilled writers, functions and audiences for writing in school, and aspects of composing such as planning and prewriting (Britton et al., 1975; Perl, 1979; Pianko, 1979).

These early studies established the recursive nature of the writing process. During their work, writers shift back and forth among the various phases of writing—composing, planning, revising, and so forth.

The writing process is not a straight superhighway from idea to finished text; it is more like a twisting mountain road with a lot of switchbacks. Unfortunately, interpretations of this body of research in elementary- and middle-school curricula in many areas did not embody the recursive characteristic of composing. Instead, it presented a picture of the writing process as a linear progression of process components from prewriting through drafting and, finally, to revising. This picture had a powerful effect on how writing instruction began to be framed.

In elementary- and middle-school classrooms a stage-bound, linear representation of writing process began being used as a model for students. Traditional instruction in which the assignment led directly to single-draft finished products began to be viewed critically, as a process model helped teachers understand the inadequacy of the assignment-to-product mode of instruction. Using the linear conception of composing (prewrite-write-revise), teachers developed myriad instructional techniques intended to make writing less frustrating and more natural.

Ironically, this model that heightened teacher and student awareness of writing as process also embodied the negative, as it became institutionalized as *the* model of writing process. In-school writing tasks at the elementary- and middle-school level began to take on a predictable format, in which all students would first prewrite, making explicit the ideas they intended to write, through such activities as brainstorming and outlining. Students then wrote the complete text based on their prewriting; only after this stage were they encouraged to revise. Dyson and Freedman (1991b) comment on the problem inherent in this format:

> Any classroom structures that demand that all students plan, write, and revise on cue or in that order are likely to run into difficulty. Writers need flexibility, and they need time to allow the subprocesses to cycle back on each other. (p. 760)

How Thinking About the Writing Process Changed

The Flower and Hayes Model

Throughout the 1980s researchers developed various models and descriptions of the writing process. Flower and Hayes (1980, 1981) were the first to propose a model of writing process grounded in the

8

field of both rhetoric and cognitive psychology (see Figure 1). Their model, generated from think-aloud accounts of college-age writers, offered a more complex look at the processes and subprocesses of writing. It was constructed to demonstrate that process elements were both recursive and interactive. The model depicted three elements of the writing process:

> *Planning*—the process of setting goals, generating ideas, and organizing ideas.

> *Translating*—the process of attending to audience, tone, style, and syntax as well as to the motor demands of producing letters and words.

> *Reviewing*—the process of considering the text and both evaluating and revising.

Figure 1
The Flower and Hayes Model

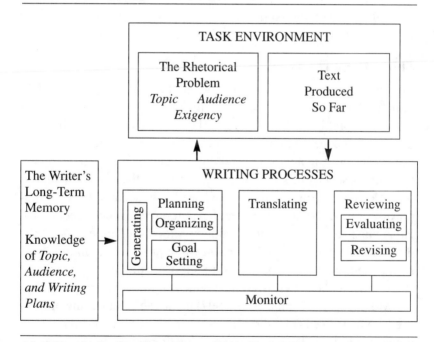

Adapted from "A Cognitive Process Theory of Writing" by L.S. Flower & J.R. Hayes, 1981, *College Composition and Communication, 32*, p. 370. Used by permission.

As an explanation of what mature writers do when they write, the description of cognitive subprocesses of these elements were particularly important. These processes interact with the *task environment*, which includes two basic elements: the rhetorical problem (What am I writing, for whom, and under what circumstances?) and the text that emerges from the writing. The process elements also interact dynamically with a writer's memory, as it works to juggle knowledge of the topic, audience awareness, and the developing plans for writing.

The model included a function called the *monitor*, which represented the writer's decisions about such things as when to generate ideas, how to organize them, and when to review. Throughout composing, the writer-as-monitor may make decisions that involve cycling back and forth through the processes.

In addition to the interactions among writing-process elements in Flower and Hayes's model, these processes also interact dynamically with a writer's long-term memory and factors connected with the writing task. The cognitive processes are not described in this model as operating in a linear order, one after another, as text is produced. On the contrary, they interrupt one another as a writer cycles back and forth among them.

Shifts From the Cognitive to the Social

The Flower and Hayes model moved the field to a far more elaborate understanding of writers' cognitive processes, but it was not without its problems. Cooper and Holzman (1989) criticized both the model and the methodology by which data were collected. Their central concern was that writing is not fundamentally a cognitive process but rather a social one structured by the shape of the environment. Explanations of writing, in their view, needed to account for the complexities of the social structure and classroom dynamics. Cooper and Holzman also questioned think-aloud protocols, commenting on the difficulty of doing a complex action while providing a running verbal account of it. They preferred to analyze composing in situated studies that looked at classroom activities and writers' processes.

More recently, Gunnarsson (1997) has argued that writing process needs to be viewed from the perspective of the communicative group doing the writing. This more sociolinguistic perspective looks at social dynamics and the way writers function as a community.

Knowledge-Telling and Knowledge-Transforming Models of Writing

Yet another way to look at writing process is to consider differing models of the ways writers generate and interact with texts. The extensive research of Bereiter and Scardamalia (1987) much of which is based on their two models of composition. These models are interesting because they attempt to explain two types of writing processes, one often used by both skilled and unskilled writers, and the other requiring a more complex interplay of thinking and writing processes seen in skilled writers. The first is represented in the *knowledge-telling* model, and the second in the *knowledge-transforming* model.

A basic assumption of the knowledge-telling model is that writing flows naturally through language abilities that human beings acquire in their everyday social experiences. According to this model, writers begin a writing task with ideas and topics identified with that task. For example, if the task were to write an essay explaining the pros and cons of school uniforms, the type of writing (explanatory) and the various topic ideas such as loss of choice, kinds of uniforms, and benefits of uniforms all would be immediately associated with the assignment. Of course, identification of the task and the topic ideas that come to the writer's mind would vary depending on the experience and sophistication of the writer. However, according to the knowledge-telling model, once the task and topics are identified, the writer retrieves information that is readily available and moves ahead in a way that "preserves the straight-ahead form of oral language production and requires no significantly greater amount of planning or goal setting than does ordinary conversation" (Bereiter & Scardamalia, 1987, p. 9). As an example, the researchers cite a self-report from a 12-year-old boy to illustrate knowledge-telling in action:

> I have a whole bunch of ideas and write down until my supply of ideas is exhausted. Then I might try to think of more ideas up to the point when you can't get any more ideas that are worth putting down on paper and then I would end it. (p. 9)

This "what next" strategy is common to young writers in the elementary grades. Without any overall plan for their writing, they tend to write from one sentence and one idea to the next, with little thought to the entire composition. This is not to say they do no monitoring of

11

their writing. The knowledge-telling model includes the idea that writers run tests of appropriateness as they write, tests that vary in sophistication with the experience of the writer (for example, attention to spelling, word choice, or structure). The writing described in this model is similar to what is often described as freewriting, a strategy commonly used as a preliminary exploration of ideas when writers are thinking about a topic. Bereiter and Scardamalia suggest that the knowledge-telling process is encouraged by freewriting, which may be counterproductive to learning how to think about a specific piece of writing as a purposeful, whole, and cohesive piece. This view is supported by Goldstein and Carr's (1996) research on data from the 1992 U.S. National Assessment of Educational Progress (NAEP), where they found that simply drafting a piece of writing was not as effective as using certain prewriting strategies.

With the knowledge-transforming model, on the other hand, a basic assumption is that during the process of writing, writers are actively transforming their thoughts. This is a phenomenon often reported among experienced writers, as we discuss in the next section of this chapter. This model depicts writing as a problem-solving process in which writers consider changes in their text while concurrently making changes in what they want to say. Their knowledge in this reflective process can be affected by the act of writing and thinking. "Thus it is that writing can play a role in the development of their knowledge" (Bereiter & Scardamalia, 1987, p. 11).

The two models do not describe two completely unrelated processes: The knowledge-telling model often may be used along with the knowledge-transforming model. For example, parts of a student draft may flow naturally from knowledge and information the writer already possesses, while other parts may involve invention or discovery of meaning as the text unfolds. The primary difference is that with the knowledge-transforming model, the writing processes involve "a two-way interaction between continuously developing knowledge and continuously developing text" (Bereiter & Scardamalia, 1987, p. 13). The knowledge-telling model presents a picture of writing processes as they function in producing text that is based on what the writer already knows. We discuss this further in the next chapter when we look at research on children's composing processes as they write in their classrooms.

Differences Between Novice and Expert Writers

In research designed to test the validity of the knowledge-telling and the knowledge-transforming models of writing process, Bereiter and Scardamalia (1987) highlight some distinct differences between novice and more expert writers. For example, in research with fifth-grade, tenth-grade, and adult writers the researchers observed the time it took for each group to begin writing after being given a storywriting cue. They observed writers' behaviors when limitations regarding time and length were imposed on the task and when no limitations were imposed.

What they found supported both the knowledge-telling and knowledge-transforming models. Regardless of the time allowed or the length requirement, fifth-grade writers began writing almost immediately (within seconds of receiving the cue), as would be expected with the knowledge-telling model. They quickly retrieved ideas and topic cues from their existing knowledge and began generating text, not unlike how one would begin and take part in a conversation. The tenth graders behaved similarly, although they did vary their start-up times for longer pieces, taking longer to begin when they were cued to write longer stories.

The adults, on the other hand, varied their writing behaviors noticeably when time and length limitations were altered. When given more time to write, they took even longer periods of time getting started. In addition, when they were asked to write longer texts, their start-up times increased. The more expert writers did not treat all writing tasks in the same manner, altering their writing behaviors in such a way that suggested they were moving from a strictly knowledge-telling to a knowledge-transforming process. The assumption is that the more expert writers were using the extra time to plan, but, as Bereiter and Scardamalia note, the nature of the thinking and planning was not clear in this research; it was only inferred from observable behaviors.

Novice and expert writers are different in their experiences and capabilities; and in writing, those differences may help explain why composing behaviors vary as writers become increasingly expert. Perhaps when we understand the differences, we can design instruction that will better support elements of writing processes for young writers as they develop.

Effects of Writing-Process Understandings on Instruction

Evidence suggests that researchers' attempts to understand and describe writing processes have had a positive impact on the teaching of writing. Data were drawn from the 1992 NAEP in the area of writing in order to explore the effect of writing-process oriented instruction on young writers' development. Goldstein and Carr (1996) examined the NAEP writing data on approximately 7,000 fourth graders, 11,000 eighth graders, and 11,500 twelfth graders, and asked the question: Can students benefit from process writing? They found the following:

- Students who were consistently encouraged by their teachers to use elements of writing process, such as planning and defining purpose and audience, tended to be better writers than students whose teachers reportedly never encouraged the use of such activities.

- Average writing ability was higher among students whose teachers consistently encouraged them to use several strategies associated with elements of writing process.

- Students who were consistently encouraged by thcir teachers to use various prewriting strategies tended to attain higher scores than other students.

There is, however, a qualifier to this last finding. Goldstein and Carr report that only those who used lists, outlines, or diagrams tended to outperform those who showed no evidence of prewriting. Students who created unrelated notes or drawings or who simply wrote first drafts performed about the same as those who did no prewriting.

Other research indicates that using writing process as a basis for instruction has a positive effect on the writing achievement of learning-disabled students. For example, the Cognitive Strategy in Writing (CSIW) program, which had been effective for elementary children with learning disabilities, was subsequently adapted for middle-school children with learning disabilities (Hallenbeck, 1995). This strategy emphasizes text structures and writing processes, using think-sheets to encourage planning, organizing, revising, and editing. For example, in the planning process, strategies employed by expert writers were used to guide think-alouds. The teacher first modeled the processes by discussing a purpose for the writing and demonstrating his own preliminary thinking and brainstorming. The teacher reviewed items from the brainstorming session by saying such things as "What else should I tell the reader about this idea that I haven't already listed?" (p. 15). He then modeled the process of organizing ideas using colored markers to categorize brainstormed ideas. These items were transferred to the organization section of the thinksheet. A concept map was created in which ideas were grouped together, and the class discussed the groupings and the rationale for each. Groups of ideas were then given titles with students' input. After the demonstration, students completed their own sheets. Hallenbeck found, using pre- and post-assessments of students' writing, that over the course of a school year student writing improved on all measures, including fluency (quantity), structure and organization, reader sensitivity, and overall quality measured by holistic scores.

Because writing is process, it is not surprising that instructional strategies that emphasize process elements would contribute to young writers' increasing proficiency. Based on current understandings, the issue is not whether process strategies enhance a writer's ability to write effectively. Rather, the issue centers on which activities and classroom structures will best address individual writers' needs in various task environments and with various writing demands.

Learning From Practicing Writers

Process-writing programs often look to the accounts of practicing authors for insights into a writer's work. In this section we sample professional writers' self-reports in an effort to consider their views of writing and think about possible implications for classroom programs.

In his book *Shoptalk: Learning to Write With Writers*, Murray (1990) presents self-reports from highly experienced and well-known writers. He groups their reports thematically around such categories as why writers write, the effect of audience on writers' work, where writers get their ideas for writing, and how they approach a writing task. In his introduction, Murray notes that writers at times contradict one another, a natural occurrence given that they talk about a wide range of writing tasks and, in addition, each brings "an individual history" to the task.

Flannery O'Connor, for example, says, "I write because I don't know what I think until I read what I say" (Murray, 1990, p. 8). Similarly, E.M. Forster's famous quotation also highlights the idea of discovery inherent in the planning-drafting interaction: "How do I know what I think until I see what I say?" (p. 101). E.L. Doctorow expresses the interaction of planning and drafting processes when he says, "I have to write every day because, the way I work, the writing generates the writing" (p. 51).

Another book, similar to Murray's, contains self-reports of writers who write fiction, nonfiction, and poetry for children and young adolescents. The book, *How Writers Write* (Lloyd, 1987), groups writers' self-reports around categories or themes and presents them in chapters such as "How and Where Writers Write," "Where Do Ideas Come From?" and "The First Draft."

In Lloyd's book, Beverly Cleary's self-report reveals what many writers of fiction express, that as she writes, the writing seems to take on a life of its own. She states, "I start with a character or an incident and begin to write, and as I write the character grows" (p. 35). Steven Kellogg says it another way: "I usually have just a small piece of an idea, or a little thought, or a little picture in my mind, and then I put that on the paper and try to let it grow in whatever way it wants to grow, to start to move" (p. 30).

On the other hand, the diversity evident in writers' self-reports is seen in Rosemary Sutcliff's comments about writing historical fiction. She describes collecting extensive information on the place and period she is writing about and then carefully copying that information into what she calls her "red exercise book." Only then does she begin to write. She reports,

> When I've got it all together, then I start writing the story. The book is fairly well shaped in my mind before I begin writing. It isn't a detailed synopsis, but I know the beginning, middle and end. I just can't start writing a book and think I'll find out how it ends later. (p. 64)

Likewise, Lloyd Alexander talks about doing extensive research for his fiction. He comments, "I do a lot of research for my stories before I start to write the first draft. In the story about the cat, called

Time Cat, I read every book about cats that I could find" (p. 70). Interestingly, however, Alexander remarks that when he is finally ready to write, he feels he has absorbed so much information from his research that, at that point, he sets the research aside and simply begins writing: "The researched information will weave naturally into the story. It's awful when the research shows in a story, because it hasn't become a natural part of the writing" (p. 71).

Jane Yolan reports the planning process somewhat differently. Planning seems to thread its way through her entire composing task, which includes times when she is not physically writing:

> I actually physically write for only an hour a day, but I'm writing my story all the time—when I'm driving the car, or taking a shower; when I first wake up in the morning, or when I am about to fall asleep. I'm thinking about ideas and processing them, and that's all part of the writing. (p. 97)

We find it intriguing that Perl's (1979) work (which, as mentioned earlier, followed Emig's study) is highly supportive of practicing writers' self-reports. Working with what she calls "unskilled college writers," Perl did not use think-aloud protocols or interviews. Instead, she attempted to code every aspect of these students' activities as they composed. She concludes that writers do invent as they write, and that they discover specific words and details, syntactic structures, and larger organizational structures:

> Composing always involves some measure of both construction and discovery. Writers construct their discourse inasmuch as they begin with a sense of what they want to write. This sense, as it remains implicit, is not equivalent to the explicit form it gives rise to.... Writers know more fully what they mean only after having written it. (p. 331)

Reports from practicing writers add to the research base and our understandings about writing processes. Their reports vary significantly, depending on many factors, including the writers themselves and the preferences they have developed through experience and the writing task. The diversity that is obvious in their collective voices is also seen in other writing-process research, where individuals appear to be influenced by their own preferences, experience, and knowledge, as well as by the writing task itself and the task environment. Each of these variables has specific implications for the classroom and the teaching of writing. In the following sections, we reflect on ways in which research has informed us, and on some questions that still need to be answered.

Classroom Implications and Ideas for Instruction

Even the most traditional writing assignment (for example, the five-paragraph theme) implies a writing process. However, processes of writing have not always been made explicit within the writing classroom. The research reviewed in this chapter suggests that when teachers help students think about and use writing strategies related to writing process, students' writing improves. Teaching writing-process strategies within the classroom benefits students with learning disabilities, as well.

A number of teaching issues apply to the use of writing processes in the classroom:

Accommodation. Because writing processes occur recursively and interact with one another, and because these processes are idiosyncratic to the writing task, the writer, and the writing environment, no two students will be at the same point in the writing process at any given time. Classroom writing routines and practices need to be flexible so that students can make the best choices about their use of writing strategies. Classroom practices such as writing workshop (discussed in Chapter 3) accommodate a group of writers working across the writing processes.

Strategies. Research demonstrates that younger children tend just to start writing without thinking through what they want to say and how they might go about organizing their message. Beginning (and struggling) writers need to have access to strategies for composing, planning, starting, and reformulating (correcting, revising, and rewriting). As writers progress, they can be encouraged to increase their repertoire of strategies and vary how they use them across writing projects. For example, teachers can encourage youngsters to make a list, using short phrases or single words, of all the ideas they associate with a topic, then organize their lists around themes or idea clusters, and finally begin drafting their text based on the ideas they have generated. Teachers may especially wish to focus on strategies that support writing as a way of transforming knowledge. For instance, projects in which students write in response to their reading or in which students write about a topic after reading two or more sources help students make concepts their own.

Methods. One of the most effective ways of teaching writing-process strategies is through demonstration. Teachers go through an aspect of the writing process (for example, the use of think-sheets) themselves in front of the students, talking out loud about what they are doing and why they are doing it. Other models of writers at work are available for students as well. There are books (for example, the Lloyd book cited earlier in this chapter) about published authors' writing processes that may be used in minilessons about strategies. Discussion of writing process can become a part of the classroom's everyday talk about writing. Finally, collaborating writers in the classroom may become models for one another demonstrating effective strategies for writing. Young writers can discuss where they get their ideas for writing, how they get started, when they revise and edit, and how they solve problems in their writing. It is important to remember that their self-reports can vary not only from student to student but also from writing task to writing task. Students can learn from one another as they share their successful strategies.

Problem Solving. An individual's writing process is complex—it is influenced by the nature of the task at hand, cognitive factors, and social factors. When there is a problem in a student's writing, the teacher may wish to consider all three of these areas in addressing the problem. For example, a writer might be reluctant because the tasks that the class is working on are not personally interesting. Alternatively, the writer might be reluctant because he or she does not know how to begin to work on the writing. Or, the writer might be reluctant because he or she is afraid that the other children might make fun of his or her writing. Each of these possibilities suggests very different approaches to addressing a writer's reluctance.

Looking Ahead

There are many factors to think about in an attempt to understand writing processes and translate those understandings to the teaching of writing. It is important to consider differences in ability and experience (novices versus experts) and differences in writing tasks. Some of the questions that remain include those on the following page.

- How can teachers help young writers come to understand their own writing processes?
- What factors help certain writers work productively?
- What are the influences of task, writing environment, and writer preferences within the classroom writing program?

In this chapter we have discussed practicing writers' self-reports and how their insights help advance our understandings about writing process. As we shift the focus to younger students, it seems important to inquire into young writers' own insights about their writing and their perspectives about writing in school. Can interviews with these young writers, as well as their reflective journals and autobiographies, provide students and their teachers with useful perspectives on writing processes, on writing tasks, and on writing instruction?

Perhaps a more basic concern related to these questions is whether young, developing writers are able to provide reliable information in their self-reports. In doctoral research conducted in 1970, Sawkins interviewed 10- and 11-year-old children about their composing. After analyzing students' interviews and observing their writing behaviors and their writings, she concluded that they were able with a high degree of reliability to articulate their composing processes. We believe that teachers are interested in what young writers know and articulate about their writing processes. What are young children's understandings as they write, and how do they change with time and experience?

The body of current research on children's writing processes does not address many of the concepts of writing that practicing writers describe. We are interested, for example, in what it means to think of writing as an act of discovery. How can instruction and classroom environments provide guidance for young writers as they engage in discovery? How much of writing is discovery, and how much must young, developing writers know before they begin writing about a chosen topic? And how much does the writing task and the demands of that task affect such decisions?

It appears that development, as well as instructional cues and processes, have potentially powerful effects on children's writing. We know that the relations between development and instruction are subtle ones. As we construct classroom programs to support young writers, we have many questions to resolve:

- What are the roles of specific instructional strategies and processes in supporting and promoting students' development as writers?
- Understanding the value of goal setting for writers, how can teachers support a young writer's goals for a particular writing project so they lead to specific plans, which will, in turn, lead to successful completion a particular writing task?
- What instructional strategies will help young writers become increasingly effective at reviewing and revising—in other words, at being critical self-evaluators of their writing?

It appears from the research that writers who have clear criteria for their writing, and whose planning results in clear intentions and expectations for a particular writing task, tend to be more effective at self-evaluating and revising. What instructional designs and strategies will support these processes, and how does the effectiveness of those strategies vary with a writer's level of development and expertise? (See Chapter 7 for a related discussion in the work of teacher researcher Cathy Boyle.)

A fundamental premise of this work, and the research that has preceded it for the past several decades, is that the more we understand the nature of children's writing processes, the dynamic interactions of these processes, and how those interactions differ among individuals, the easier it will be to design instructional environments that support children and their individual needs as they grow and develop in their writing abilities.

CHAPTER 2

The Writing Processes of Children

Writing teachers and researchers are especially concerned with the way that children's writing develops as they grow older. A first grader and an eighth grader occupy completely different worlds, and this is particularly true in terms of each student's writing. How do children move from novice writers in the primary grades to skilled writers who have developed the multiple competencies that many middle-school students possess? How might teachers help support this writing development?

The focus in this chapter is on what children do when they write, that is, children's writing processes in school settings. Selected studies of children's writing are discussed by grade levels (primary, intermediate, and middle school) in order to reveal emerging patterns of writing development. The chapter also highlights the implications of particular studies for classroom instruction. In addition, we reflect on what selected studies do and do not tell those of us who work with children in classroom writing programs.

Children's Composing Processes

Like the practicing writers cited in Chapter 1, when children in our classrooms write, their processes involve not only their strategies for producing their intended works, but also their visions of what they are constructing, sense of themselves as writers within the classroom culture, and understanding of written language. Children's past writing instruction and environmental factors such as experiences and beliefs in the home and community all influence what they do and think as they write.

As mentioned in Chapter 1, a number of key studies support the idea that children's writing in school is affected by the social and cultural contexts in which writing takes place and also by the classroom learning activities in which children participate (Dyson, 1989, 1991). We know that children try to determine what teachers value or consider significant. Children monitor what teachers talk about in classroom writing demonstrations and the teacher's responses to the writings of others. They also assess the peer culture and know what counts or gets attention within the classroom world of child writers. All of these contextual values shape the decisions children make as they write.

Children's Writing in the Primary Grades

Writing-as-Play

One of the early studies of primary grade children's writing processes was Donald Graves's 1975 work. His analyses of second graders' actions showed that their composing often begins during the process of sketching or working with crayons. A meaning or story may emerge or be discovered within these processes of exploration.

In 1981 Graves and his colleagues undertook an extensive study that spanned two years and two groups of children. One group of eight children was observed from the beginning of first grade to the end of second grade, and a second group of eight was observed from the beginning of third grade through fourth grade. Their research included direct observations of students as they wrote; interviews with children before, during, and after their writing; and analyses of written products. As children composed, researchers would sit alongside the young writer, taking notes and asking questions. In addition, researchers observed and took notes as the children talked with their peers and their teachers about writing.

Based on this research, Graves (1981) defines children's writing process as "a series of operations leading to the solution of a problem. The process begins when the writer consciously or unconsciously starts a topic and is finished when the written piece is published" (p.

4). Graves emphasizes the idea that composing can begin before the physical process of writing actually begins. He also identifies sub-processes associated with writing, such as topic selection, rehearsing, accessing information, paying attention to spelling and handwriting, reading, organizing, editing, and revising, and concluded that the same process elements were evident whether the children were 6 or 10 years old.

With the youngest writers, Graves and his colleagues found that the decision to write was often spontaneous, perhaps sparked by a desire to write a caption on their own picture. For 6-year-olds, the composing process tends to begin with the spontaneous decision to write and to end when the child fashions the letters to compose a caption. Graves concludes that in such circumstances, "process resembles spontaneous play" (p. 7).

The idea of writing-as-play is evident in numerous aspects of young children's writing. They experiment with letters, words, spacing, and writing materials. They are secure that they are communicating meaning and are eager to tell their written message to a reader, who may not know what the writing says. Graves remarks that the egocentricity of these young writers "has its own protective cloak" (p. 179). As they develop, however, these children begin to realize that they themselves are not always sure what has been written. Their teachers and peers have questions about what they write, and the children begin to realize that their writing must be able to communicate beyond the moment in which the writing occurred. They understand that they are not always available to explain their work to a reader and that the writing must be able to stand on its own.

Graves and his colleagues also note that young children tend to employ what Bereiter and Scardamalia (1987) called the "what next" strategy. Children move from one piece of information to another, not planning ahead but instead, writing from one idea to the next, confident that they are clearly expressing their meaning.

Among the youngest writers in Graves's (1981) study, much of the writing process is visible or overt. They talk about what they are going to write and often talk their way through a writing. This latter process may serve various purposes; perhaps they are hearing the sounds within a word so they can decide which letters to select. The children reread aloud what they have written, almost as though they were cycling back to check meaning and get a running start into what will come next.

The Emergence of Planning From Writing-as-Play

Although children's earliest writings seem to be spontaneous and unplanned, as their writing develops, evidence of planning and rehearsal of ideas prior to actual writing begins to appear. Speaking aloud before and during composing disappears. The emphasis seems to shift from talking out the ideas and focusing on handwriting and spelling to focusing on context. Children are increasingly able to select information for their writing without having to overtly rehearse or discuss the possibilities. For example, Cioffi (1984), who conducted case studies focusing on two first graders, discovered that over the course of the two years one of the students decreased the time he spent composing orally (saying each word aloud as he wrote it and drawing pictures to illustrate) from a median of about 77% of his composing time to a median of 22%. Silent writing, on the other hand, increased from 0% to 57% of the composing time. Cioffi found a similar trend with the other student in his study, although the changes were not so dramatic in her writing.

Early Integration of Reading and Writing

Research documenting the writing actions of first graders in classrooms that emphasize the integration of reading and writing show that those experiences play a role in children's early writing processes. For instance, Dahl and Freppon (1995) observed inner-city first graders reading and writing across the first-grade year and found that writers in urban first grades considered their reading experiences as sources of topics and structures for writing. They copied from favorite books and used stories read by the teacher to suggest story patterns for writing. Children used the trade books in their classroom library for themes, genre information, character ideas, or general story support. They sometimes looked up the spellings of specific words in familiar storybooks. Experiences with the language of trade books led to production of original works with the language choices and structures learned from reading. (See Chapter 5 for more about relations between reading and writing.)

Writing as Exploration

For the learners mentioned in the preceding paragraph and for primary-grade children in other studies, play also served as a way of exploring and transforming ideas when children were writing. Children played with language and its sounds and spellings. Role playing and collaborative play generated and extended ideas for writing and helped child writers make decisions about stories. These child-initiated playful interactions occurred spontaneously when young writers were free to explore meanings and interpret their experience through writing.

In MacGillivray's (1994) qualitative research describing a year with first-grade writers, she shows that children write in three broad categories: here and now, the past, and fantasy. In addition, she found that the first graders in her study held some writing values in common. For example, keeping the audience's interest and being able to read their own writing, regardless of spelling, were most important. Also, some children used writing as an act of unity to resolve peer issues, while others used writing as a way of joining peers in collaboration, or to explore self and the world. Clearly, for these young children, writing was important for a variety of reasons.

Research by Dyson

Within the body of research on primary-grade writers, the works of Ann Haas Dyson have been particularly prominent. Although a systematic review of her research is beyond the scope of this chapter, we have chosen key works that describe some fundamental concepts about children's writing processes.

TWO PRIMARY-GRADE CASE STUDIES. In *Multiple Worlds of Child Writers*, Dyson (1989) presents case studies of what young writers do when they compose and describes the principles underlying children's development as they discover and express meanings. Over a period of two years she observed four children's talk, drawing, and writing. Her fieldnotes recorded what children were talking about with their friends, how they were using language, how they constructed meaning in art and writing, and what their written products revealed. As a sample, we briefly describe two of her four case studies.

Regina was described as a kindergarten child who lived deep within her own imaginary world, constructing imaginary characters and events as she depicted them in her drawing. She talked to herself about her drawings, providing an elaborate account of what the drawn characters were doing and saying, yet her dictations (the actual writing) did not reflect those elaborate stories in kindergarten. In first grade her pictures were gradually integrated with the written story itself, and Regina changed from a writer working in isolation within an imaginary world to one increasingly aware of her work (what she was writing and drawing) and its relation to the work of her peers. She liked to compete in spelling with her friends. Her written stories moved beyond the scope of her pictures as she related what was imagined with what she knew from her real-world experience. Eventually, her texts became ways of expressing meanings and, at the same time, forging relationships with friends.

Jake was described as a first-grade writer who also used drawing as a preliminary playful process for discovering his story or topic. He talked with other writers about his pictures and stories. Early in first grade he struggled with reading and mostly memorized his written texts rather than attempting to reread them. His slowness in writing the words he needed meant that only a small amount of text was available for others to comment on. Friends asked if the stories were real and challenged whether they went with the drawings he produced. In second grade Jake wrote about and drew pictures of an invented kind of car that was propelled by blowing bubbles. His ongoing bubble car adventures served as a story script that provided a basic structure and vocabulary for his writing. He rehearsed his story scripts through oral storytelling and sound effects during drawing and developed into a highly social craftsman of adventure stories.

Across these and other case studies, Dyson illustrates the tensions between children's imaginations and experiences (the world they know) and the written language conventions needed to communicate their meanings (the word). According to Dyson's research (1989, 1991), young writers experiment with symbol systems and ways to represent meaning as they learn about the forms and functions of written language. This means that children are grappling with the symbolic function of written language (How do I show my meaning?) while experimenting with its social function (Will my friends like this story?).

AN EXPANDED CONCEPTION OF WRITING DEVELOPMENT. Dyson's (1993a, 1995) research suggests that children across the primary grades are learning the social and personal power of print. They are creating their personal system for generating and encoding written text. They are learning not only about their own purposes and meanings in writing, but also about the expectations and needs of others. These push/pull relations between *symbolic form* and *social function* and between the *self* and *others* are tensions that undergird children's writing development.

More traditional views of writing development have traced children's growing control of spelling and of print conventions such as capital letters, punctuation, and forming paragraphs. This informative body of research on development has helped teachers interpret these aspects of children's knowledge, but not the notions about writing development that Dyson explores. Dyson is suggesting that children are constructing the rules of written language for themselves as they engage in making meaning. The central focus in writing, she contends, is developing comprehensive systems for writing across symbol systems (written language and art) and social contexts. This research-based view challenges teachers to think broadly about writing growth and consider the social and communicative factors affecting writing development.

SOCIAL AND CULTURAL DIMENSIONS FOR THE PRIMARY GRADES. The research conducted by Dyson also addresses the social and cultural contexts that influence what and how children write. Children in the primary grades must deal with their place in the social world of the classroom, the social possibilities of who they are and how they can establish themselves as individuals in that particular setting. Their development is linked to participation as social members of the writing classroom and as participants in the peer culture. The following concepts are presented in Dyson's research (1992, 1994):

1. Children use the cultural information they know from movies, cartoons, videos, and neighborhood observations in their writing. Rather than separating the cultural material from home, school, and community, children use it as elements for writing.

2. Writing purposes from a child's perspective may differ widely from more traditional school-centered notions. Writing may

be a "ticket" for peer approval; its topics, language choices, and forms are shaped by what is valued within the child collective. Children position themselves within that collective through their writing.

3. The relationships that children develop within the writing classroom are sometimes shaped by gender and race. Peer pressures are reflected in assigned roles as children act out their writing. They also are present in the roles children assign to others through their writing.

Composing Processes of Intermediate-Grade Writers

Writing With Expanded Resources

Although the documentation of primary-grade children's ways of writing is fairly extensive, the composing research portraying intermediate children is relatively scant. Calkins (1994) describes intermediate-grade writers as children who may attempt to write something significant or important. They are learners who are gradually gaining not only self-awareness, but increased deliberateness in their writing. Intermediate-grade writers draw on multiple sources of information as they write, including friends who make suggestions about their work, current and past teachers of writing, and personal experiences from their own work in the writing classroom. They are writers with repertoires of knowledge.

As children shift in self-consciousness and expand the kinds of writing they attempt in the intermediate grades, it is particularly important to understand the roles that writing plays for individual learners. McGinley and Kamberelis (1996) in their research with third and fourth graders describe the functions that writing and reading serve in a classroom. Their study used weekly observations across the school year, student and teacher interviews, participation in collaborative writing activities, and field notes of composing in classroom activities. The researchers found that as children expand their writing repertoires, they write most frequently about personal experience, using writing to consider or envision possible selves, think about personal interests, and participate in the worlds of imaginary characters.

In this study, intermediate-grade children used writing as an arena for personal exploration and growth. These young writers wrote about social problems and reflected on social action and their own identities. These findings highlight the important role the classroom reading and writing experiences play in helping young learners examine personal possibilities.

Research by Langer

Within the body of research on intermediate-grade writers, the research of Judith Langer has been particularly significant. Langer investigated the strategies and structures of children's writing and reading and described the ways that children, ages 8, 11, and 14, compose and construct meaning. We focus on the writing segment of her investigation. The method of gathering process information in Langer's (1986a) study included examining children's think-alouds on specific writing tasks. Langer focused on children's writing strategies and asked a sample of children to retrace their thinking after completing a writing task and provide a retrospective account. Children retraced their writing line by line to remember what they were thinking when they were engaged in writing. She also used interviews to explore children's ideas about what it takes to write and asked them to describe their purposes for writing.

Langer's analysis of the writing-process data shows that intermediate-grade children place a primary focus on content, on the ideas and linkages within the set of meanings they are constructing. This means that these children are primarily thinking about and manipulating concepts and considering connections among ideas. Their running accounts of composing show that they are aware of the strategies they use to get at meaning. They think about what to say next in their writing and what to include about the topic, and they make meta-comments about content and about surface features of text—whether the sentences are choppy or certain punctuation is needed.

In general, intermediate children's writing strategies indicate four broad categories of writing activity:

Generating ideas—becoming aware of relevant ideas and organizing them.

Formulating meaning—developing the message is itself a consideration of audience. Constructing the language and linking the

concepts.

Evaluating—reviewing the message constructed and monitoring its development.

Revising—restructuring, thinking about meaning, and considering where meaning has broken down.

These strategies do not proceed in linear order. Both generating and revising occur at any time during children's composing. The writer seems to step back to generate new ideas in order to move the piece forward with new content. In general, Langer's research indicates that intermediate-grade writers use strategies that help them make sense of the content about which they are writing.

Composing Processes of Middle-Grade Writers

Before addressing the body of research on middle-grade writers we turn to Nancie Atwell's description of adolescents in the writing classroom. In her award-winning book *In the Middle: Writing, reading, and learning with adolescents* Atwell (1986) includes three themes that describe adolescent writers:

1. Middle-school writers are volatile and intensely social. Their behavior is marked by confusion, bravado, restlessness, and a preoccupation with peers.

2. They are people who are growing intellectually and who want to know.

3. They need to participate in classrooms that move them toward an adult reality. They need more independent activity, increased responsibility for their own learning. and increased voice in what happens in the classroom. (p. 25)

The body of research describing the composing processes of middle-school writers suggests that these years are important ones developmentally. Bereiter and Scardamalia (1987) report that the planning process gradually becomes differentiated from text production among writers at the middle-school level. The distinctive characteristic of adolescent writers, they contend, is that planning becomes an object of contemplation in its own right. Planning helps writers sort out organization, set goals for writing, and consider strategies for shaping compositions. In a study with writers from Grades 4, 6, and 8, children's preliminary writing in the form of notes was studied in relation to their subsequent drafts. Results showed that planning and production for the fourth-grade writer were the same process. However, the planning notes of middle-school students differed from the text they generated. Their ideas (listed in notes) were later transformed and worked into the text. Their think-aloud protocols showed a marked increase in talk about planning. It thus appears that middle school may be a time when writers consider planning as increasingly important. This research was conducted with expository texts and with assigned topics. Further research may help determine whether these patterns also hold when children choose the topic and genre for their writing.

The research by Langer (1986a) on composing processes also included 14-year-olds and described the ways middle-school children go about writing both stories and reports. Langer's analysis of composing think-alouds showed that ninth graders reflect on ideas before and after writing.

To illustrate the shifts in writer attention during composing, we next discuss the before, during, and after writing patterns, then discuss the recursive nature of these processes.

Before: Fourteen-year-old writers are primarily concerned with hypothesizing prior to writing. In other words, they are reflecting on what might go into a given piece.

During: During drafting they show concern with the way the piece is developing. They divide their time among content goals, audience concerns, management of genre, and word choices. They are aware of their need to refine writing in light of what they are trying to accomplish.

After: After drafting, their comments focus on evaluation and revision of their developing text worlds. They are interested in extending and refining the ideas on paper.

Middle-school writers work back and forth in their drafts across these processes as they consider various choices and generate new possibilities. It appears that they are moving to more complex ways of composing and to increasingly differentiated understandings of genre and text structure. The studies on composing behaviors for this group do not extend across various kinds of writing programs or across subject areas.

Research needs to document the ways middle-school writers compose in various classroom settings and for various writing purposes.

Classroom Implications and Ideas for Instruction

One challenge of teaching writing is that writing is fundamentally a form of social interaction among people, and each human being has different ideas about communicating and reasons to communicate. The research sampled in this chapter reveals that as children grow from primary through intermediate and middle school, their interests and reasons for communication shift, requiring an equivalent shift in instructional techniques.

A further challenge is that writing is a complicated array of processes and subprocesses. It involves techniques at many levels, from merely forming the letters; to getting words on the page; to coping with conventions of spelling, grammar, and genre; to crafting written language, not only for meaning, but also for its aesthetic qualities.

Unfortunately, "one size fits all" writing assignments ignore the communicative function of writing and focus solely on technique. The job for teachers is to help students learn technique in the context of authentic communication.

Communication takes place in a number of contexts—as a part of problem solving, as an aspect of play, and as cultural material assembled from multiple sources by both older children and young adults beginning to explore and wanting to present themselves to the world at large. Each of these contexts for communication offers authentic possibilities for writing. In the paragraphs that follow we describe some ways that each of these three contexts for communicating in writing can be explored.

Problem solving. The research sampled in this chapter defines problem solving broadly. For example, when a child sets out to write, he or she is solving a problem, whether that problem came from within or was presented to the child by another person. Among the students who constitute a class, problems are bound to arise—not just interpersonal conflicts, but the problem of understanding other people or of struggling to present and clarify one's own ideas. Teachers can encourage children to use writing as a way of working with these problems. Through writing, children can capture and reflect on their own ideas. These personal reflections can remain private or be shared with others in collaborative problem solving.

Play. Encouraging young children to write as a form of play can be as simple as bringing writing materials into the dramatic play activities within the classroom. Teachers might use classroom drama as a source of playful writing. Children can write within the roles they take on, entering a story they have read, or write to play out ideas about a plot or a character.

Bringing together multiple materials. Teachers can encourage children to use many kinds of materials as take-off points for writing: favorite books, materials from popular culture (television, videos, newspapers, movies), and materials from home. These materials may prompt various kinds of writing: for example, children writing stories from familiar plots, commentaries about specific events or issues, or reviews of a new video or movie.

Self. Writing as a way of defining self can be supported through personal narrative and through correspondence with people outside of the classroom. Pen-pal projects are one example—particularly when the pen pals have an opportunity to meet each other, as with cross-grade pen pals in the same or neighboring school. Children can also write about family knowledge and traditions that they value, special events, or certain items that hold special meanings, such as a grandmother's rocking chair or an old box used for collecting coins.

An increasing skill and confidence in writing comes as children write to communicate. The work of Dyson and others who study young writers demonstrates that children shift their writing toward conventionality as they begin to recognize that nonconventional writing fails to communicate. Children need opportunities to make these discoveries, and instructors must celebrate and discuss students' writing actively. The works of peer authors as well as those of widely published authors provide not only a springboard for writing, but also a source of writing techniques that might solve a young writer's particular writing problems.

Looking Ahead

The body of research on children's composing at each of the three levels (primary, intermediate, and middle school) provides a beginning baseline of knowledge about writing and enables us to raise questions for future research. Current descriptions of primary-grade children engaged in composing focus on the symbol systems (words and pictures) that children use, as well as children's writing strategies and sources of information. These studies show the impact of drawing, play, and drama as children in the primary grades learn to write. Although this research clearly indicates that writing is a social event and that children's culture and peer relationships strongly influence their early writing, we still have many gaps in our knowledge about writing in the early grades. We need to know how composing in the primary grades is affected by different classroom programs and what classroom activities help children who have difficulty with writing.

As we look at research addressing the intermediate grades, it is clear that little has been written about writing in content-area classes. We need to explore the relation between children's growth in content knowledge and their writing in areas such as science, social studies, and mathematics. We also need further documentation of children's composing processes in the intermediate grades, documentation that includes information about the ways that writing is best encouraged and supported in various classroom contexts. In addition, we raise the following questions: What are the developmental benchmarks or indicators of progress for intermediate-grade writers? What role does collaboration play in the writing of children in the intermediate grades? What issues of gender and culture are reflected in the composing processes of these children?

Research on middle-school writers shows an increase of planning and genre development. We see that middle-school writers move to more complex composing strategies and juggle concerns for audience, content, genre, and structure as they generate their writing. We know that young adolescents are intensely social, but we do not have research documentation of the connections between the social dynamics in the middle-school classroom and their composing processes. Our questions include the following: What is the impact of various social and cultural dynamics on the writing of middle-school children? What gender differences are evident in adolescents' writing? How does composing differ across subject areas?

We clearly need a body of research that addresses the writing problems faced by individual learners in today's classrooms. There is scant research focused on the children who struggle in writing classrooms across the grades; on linguistically diverse writers; on children who, despite all efforts, do not grasp letter-sound relations; on children who are disinterested in writing; and on special-needs children mainstreamed into writing classrooms. We need research that investigates the supportive experiences and learner initiatives that help these children learn to write.

A substantial body of research is needed to document the interplay between teaching and learning in classroom writing programs across the grades and to describe the composing processes of children as they engage in various kinds of writing experiences. Our sense of children's growth as writers must draw on teaching-learning documentation in situated studies that describe teachers and children at work. To that end, we call for teachers to share their stories about children's writing development and conduct focused investigations that document children's writing growth in classroom writing programs. Our knowledge of children's composing must be augmented with research that explores the writing of children over time in relation to instruction and within the social and cultural contexts of the classroom.

Chapter 3

New Directions for Writing Workshop Programs

More than a decade after examinations of the initial writing workshop programs were published, it is important to look at new directions and program refinements that relate to writing workshops and instruction that supports writing processes. This chapter focuses on a selection of studies related to writing workshop programs. The investigations address some of the questions that teachers often raise, including: How can writing workshops be simplified? What should we write on student papers? How can conferences with young writers be most effective? What happens when children work together on their writing? What are the criticisms of and problems associated with workshops? What suggestions do critics offer?

Studies of Writing Workshop

An Interview with Donald Graves

On the tenth anniversary of his book *Writing: Teachers and Children at Work* (1983), Donald Graves talked about his changing focus in research and new thinking about writing workshops (Newkirk, 1994). His research interests had moved from trying to document sequences of children's writing development to looking at the conditions for learning within literate classrooms. In the interview, Graves suggests that valuable information about writing comes from noticing children's learning, listening to their talk, and examining one's own literate practices. In rethinking the concept of writing workshops after a decade of work, he reconsiders the central role of writing conferences in providing instruction for children, contending that significant instruction in writing also comes through the social interactions among children and their independent experimentation with writing. He suggests that writing classrooms move from fixed routines or orthodoxies to focused attention on learning. This means, for example, noticing the circumstances, such as topic choices and social dynamics, when students are deeply engaged and writing productively. Graves also emphasizes the importance of slowing down in instructional programs and crafting classroom environments in order to allow children to talk, experiment, and explore writing.

New Directions in Process-Writing Instruction

In contrast to the original pioneering works about process-writing instruction (Atwell, 1987; Calkins, 1986; Graves, 1983), new works expand their explanations of genre exploration with elementary- and middle-school writers. Calkins (1994) describes comprehensive genre studies in which children are immersed in reading, studying, and writing in specific genres over time. She outlines instruction in literary nonfiction, poetry, memoirs, and theme studies as ways of expanding children's writing experiences. Graves (1994) discusses teaching actions that help teachers gain insights into writing workshop instruction. Harwayne (1992) builds specific linkages to a literature program and weaves together children's writing experiences and their study of specific literary works. Atwell's (1990) collection of teacher research presents intermediate-grade teachers' explorations of report writing, notetaking, literary logs, and journals as classroom practices expanding children's experiences with writing across various subject areas.

Recent works on writing workshops also show an expansion of information about the craft of writing. These books include material about what writers do, what issues writers grapple with, and how writers work. For example, in *What a Writer Needs* (Fletcher, 1993) there are descriptions about the ways that writers in the elementary and middle grades handle issues such as time, focus, settings, characterizations, and tension within their pieces.

The number of teacher-authored books about writing has increased recently. These references offer extensive information about the management of writing workshop programs at specific grade levels and expand the existing information about process writing with detailed program descriptions and extensive listings of resources (Avery, 1993; Fraser & Skolnick, 1994; Rief, 1993). In the remainder of this chapter, we discuss these new works and the emerging body of research about children's writing within workshop programs.

Conferences With Young Writers in Writing Workshop Contexts

Conferences pose a host of problems for teachers in writing workshop programs. Beyond the matter of finding time for conferences and managing the rest of the class, the main concern is how to talk to writers about their work in ways that teach and inspire more writing. Some researchers say that conferences are scaffolds for student revision or for specific skill instruction; others see conferences as ways of focusing a writer's attention—a personal conversation that provides an informed audience and poses critical questions. Freedman and Sperling (1985) describe one view of conferences: "Characterized by turn taking, the conference-as-conversation also allows each participant to raise issues, to shift topics, and to encourage or discourage elaboration" (p. 107). These authors claim that conferences are shaped by differences in authority between teacher and student as well as by the teacher's overall agenda of imparting new knowledge to individual learners.

Newkirk (1995) also suggests (for writers who are college students) that conferences may be performances that are influenced by the roles that participants play. The demands of performance shape how a conference is supposed to go and how participation is interpreted. Student writers whose answers are too brief or who are silent may be thought to perform less well than those playing the role and taking extended turns.

Whether these performance roles played by older writers also hold true for younger ones in individual conferences has not been investigated. Writing conferences at the elementary- and middle-school level feature the give and take of teaching-learning events; young writers respond to this event in many ways, occasionally resisting teacher recommendations.

We highlight three studies that provide ideas about conferences. The first is a study by Fitzgerald and Stamm (1992), who analyzed small-group conferences with the teacher and looked at the changes in writing of particular first-grade students. The second study by McCarthey (1994) focuses on individual teacher-student conferences in a fifth- and sixth-grade classroom. The third study looks at how teachers adjust their verbal responses in conferences to meet the needs of various students.

Small-Group Conferences

The teacher in the Fitzgerald and Stamm study guided small-group conferences with three questions: What was the piece about? What did you like about it? and What comments or suggestions do you have for the author? She contributed suggestions for revision along with those suggested by children.

The researchers wanted to know what influence these conferences had on revision knowledge and revision activity. They collected conference transcripts every other week for the last half of the school year in first grade and interviewed children about the changes they wanted to make in their pieces. The researchers kept track of the revisions that two selected case-study children made, noting their relation to revisions recommended in group conferences.

The researchers selected for their case studies a knowledgeable first-grade writer with a record of extensive revising, and a relatively inexperienced first-grade writer who understood how to revise but engaged in few actual revisions. The researchers observed several group conferences with the teacher and each learner's successive writing efforts.

Interestingly, the knowledgeable writer tended to ignore the teacher and writing group's revision recommendations. Despite a high level of independent revision activity, he tended to revise less after group conferences. The less experienced writer, in contrast, tended to follow conference suggestions and consistently made recommended revisions. It appeared that, for the second young writer, the group conferences provided a specific direction for change and a way to explore possible revisions. This learner in turn explored revision on her own and showed a growing sophistication in the kinds of revisions that she made.

The Fitzgerald and Stamm study suggests that learners make choices as they participate in writing conferences. Participation in the group conference is not merely a matter of learning what one is required to do. Instead, ownership of writing and at-the-moment interests influence student decisions about whether to follow through on recommendations. Moreover, the less skilled writer's conferences served as direct scaffolds showing how and where to revise. Evidence in this second case shows that the conference enabled the writer to explore her already existing, if unexplored, interest in revision.

Individual Conferences

The second study, about individual conferences, is a controversial one. McCarthey focused on synchrony, how "in tune" conference participants were with each other and how productive the teacher-student conferences were in terms of helping writers learn to make changes in their writing. The teacher in this study was specific about recommended changes and adamant about the goals of her writing instruction. In contrast to process-writing notions of writer autonomy, her view of conferences included writer compliance with recommendations that were settled on in the give and take of the conference. Over a 5-week period of observing, videotaping, and recording conferences, McCarthey studied the match between specific recommendations and children's revisions. She interviewed the teacher about what she was trying to do, her goals, and information about students. She informally interviewed fifth- and sixth-grade students about conferences, their own texts and revisions, and where they got their ideas. Each student in the study also conducted a writing conference with a first-grade student and talked about that student's writing. These student-directed conferences were used to see what the older learners had learned about writing.

The four case studies of fifth- and sixth-grade writers in this particular classroom showed that finding common ground in conferences involved talking about and implementing major changes that the teacher strongly recommended. Three of the four students were able to transform teacher recommendations into writing changes by drawing on their understanding of the teacher's ideas about writing and accepting the teacher's requirements for specific writing tasks. Not only did students use the teacher's ideas about writing and make them their own, they drew from those ideas later in the conferences with younger children.

One of the four case-study students did not conform to this pattern. In this case, the child was new to writing workshop routines, the teacher and student did not have a good relationship, and the child's work was not viewed as good writing by the teacher. There was conflict in conferences; in one, the topic the student chose did not fit the teacher's image of a good text, and the teacher talked about an alternative topic that matched the assignment. Unfortunately, the task involved writing about one's father and, unbeknownst to the teacher, that was a painful topic for the child. The child's dilemma was how to please the teacher and not write about a painful subject, and the writer was unsuccessful in the writing task and in the subsequent conference.

McCarthey's case studies provoke questions about writing conferences in classrooms and about research designs that interpret classroom practices. Researchers criticized the short period of time for data gathering and the disapproving view taken toward the teacher. The study, as a whole, posed difficult questions for the field: What is the relation between the teacher's image of a good text and an emerging writer's ideas? How do conferences best support student learning and also bolster writer independence? What provisions are there for children who are not adept at thinking and talking about writing processes and strategies and not skilled at working toward a common ground with the teacher? The need for classroom research about these aspects of teaching is particularly critical as teachers attempt to refine and reevaluate conference practices with children across age and ability levels.

Teachers' Discourse in Conferences

The third study we have selected addresses the issue of how teachers adjust their talk in conferences for different learners and what options are available to help teachers in this context. In order to document conference practices, McCredie, Vukelich, and Roe (1996) analyzed one teacher's shifting conversational strategies. Analyses of several conferences with two contrasting writers showed the teacher adjusting strategies for specific learners. One 8-year-old writer, adept at process talk, responded as the teacher asked her questions, suggested options, and gave her opportunities to make choices. This writer, able to self-evaluate suggestions and maintain ownership of her writing, used conferences to gain additional information about her pieces and extend her insights about writing options. The teacher's conversational strategies were akin to traditional scaffolding moves that help the writer discover and evaluate possible changes from an array of choices. For example, when the young writer was bored with writing a long story, the teacher suggested ways to cut it into a serialized version by ending at a point when the suspense was at its highest. For another piece the teacher simply asked questions that helped the writer consider different options for the story ending. The young writer used her own answers as she made decisions about the piece.

These same strategies were not successful with a second 8-year-old who was less comfortable with conference talk and saw each teacher suggestion as evidence that she, as a writer, was "messing up." In a shift of strategies, the teacher created a visible scaffold for this student. The teacher asked the writer to dictate key elements of the story in response to her questions, and she wrote them on separate notecards for the child. The teacher-written cards that were produced as they talked through the prospective story then were used independently by the young writer to organize and extend her piece. The teacher's role was that of an active helper or collaborator, and the strategy showed the writer how to proceed.

This shift in approaches suggests the importance of continued exploration of conference strategies for various learners. It also reminds us that we do not have sufficient research about conference alternatives with differing writers at various grade levels. The field has moved beyond the one-size-fits-all mold, but it needs critical examinations of various conference alternatives.

Writers Working Together

When young writers work together, the issue is whether they can provide real help for one another and whether they will stay on task. The studies in this area describe peer relationships in writing workshop settings: the social dynamics among children and the construction of peer cultures, as well as the ways that peers function in writing groups and in conference pairs.

Children's writing is linked to the social milieu, that is, to the surrounding world of talk and peer values. Dyson's research shows that children's ideas as writers are influenced by the ways that peers work together and the social values of the child collective. They are "expressing who they are among other people" (Dyson, 1989, p. 276) in their acts of talking and writing. (See Hudson, 1986, and Schultz,

1994, for additional research on children's writing and the social contexts of the classroom.)

Our search for studies about peer responses and peer conferences shows that a large portion of the research relates to older writers at the secondary and college level (DiPardo & Freedman, 1988). A study by Gere and Abbott (1985) serves as an example of the few studies that include elementary- and middle-school children. This study investigated writing groups at the fifth-, eighth-, and eleventh-grade levels, analyzing what writers talked about and what kinds of help peers provided. Their results were positive: Peers functioned effectively, stayed on task, and talked about content and process. Such productive group talk among peers, the authors suggested, may enable writers to become more aware of their processes as writers.

Yet, peer conferences may not always be constructive. Lensmire (1994), working as a teacher researcher in his third-grade classroom, followed the peer relationships and writing progress in his classroom. He collected extensive field notes; kept detailed records of lesson plans, rules, and procedures; audiotaped workshop sessions; made arrangements for his students to be interviewed at year's end by colleagues who agreed to help collect data; and analyzed students' writings throughout the year. As the year unfolded, he became increasingly aware of the powerful role that social context was playing in workshop settings. Several students' fictionalized writings became not-so-veiled attacks on less-popular students. Teasing among boys and girls found subtle voice through their writings. Students resisted many genres and topics, preferring fictionalized narratives, which did not demand as much personal sharing and, thus, risk taking.

Lensmire found that the social outliers of the group were mistreated by their peers within the writing workshop setting. Some children took the brunt of peer cruelty in response to their writing like they took teasing on the playground or ridicule in the cafeteria. Jessie, a child who lived in a trailer park, described her feelings to the interviewer:

Interviewer: What would they do with your writing? How would you feel if you had to conference with them?

Jessie: I would feel like a jar of slime. Being sat on.

Interviewer: So maybe they don't treat you very well?

Jessie: Yes. No like getting cut in half. (p. 78)

Jessie's negative feelings suggest the urgency of close monitoring of conferences and sharing experiences. They also point to the possible tensions that young writers may feel as they write for an audience of peers. The assumption that children are supported by these peer-oriented experiences may be wrong for some workshop participants. Perhaps children with many friends have a far easier time in peer conferences than outsiders who are writing within a climate that denies peer support. Lensmire reminds us that writers may lose their willingness to write if they bend to peer audiences at the cost of their own ideas.

Other factors such as gender and race also may surface as issues in writing classrooms and may cause conflicts as children share and hold conferences about their writing. For example, Finders (1996) traces the literate underlife of junior high girls by looking at two social cliques, the Social Queens and the Tough Cookies. The tensions between friendship group membership and participation in classroom reading-writing workshop shows that adolescent girls may limit their participation to conform to peer-group standards. For example, membership in the Tough Cookies carried with it restrictions on publicly sharing ideas for writing and limitations on group members' topic choices. An interview statement shows the conflict with official expectations:

> *Cleo:* I hate it when you have to share ideas in a group. People can steal your ideas. If anyone gets me an idea, I have to reject it. It has to be mine. I don't share my real ideas. (p. 109)

These rules of the social clique tend to privilege the private and marginalize the public, thus making writing workshop participation problematic. This research and other studies about gender and racial interpretations of self in school alert us to the differences between student and adult perspectives in the day-to-day workings of the writing workshop and the need to critically evaluate and rethink classroom practices.

Finders makes several recommendations for middle-school teachers making an effort to support students in their writing and bring a sociocultural perspective into the classroom. She advocates a student-negotiated pedagogy that acknowledges social and cultural dynamics and suggests creating social spaces where differing cultures may deal with one another, perhaps using writing to investigate their differences. She advocates explicitly acknowledging the silences and voices that are motivated politically. In sum, she advocates adding layers of critical reflection to a student-centered curriculum.

Writing Workshop Revisited

The intent in a revisiting of writing workshop is to view it as a dynamic and changing conception of writing instruction and to explore new directions suggested through research. Earlier in this chapter we described some of the findings from Lensmire's (1994) ethnography of writing workshop in his third-grade classroom. His research resulted in several insights about workshop procedures and teachers' roles. One insight has to do with the types of writing brought to workshop settings. Lensmire suggests that workshops might work better if students work collectively toward a common goal or purpose. For example, a class might collectively study a particular genre through reading and writing. Through such study, texts are seen as "'problems to be solved'—either in the production of certain genres of texts, or in the reading, interpretation, and criticism of texts" (p. 155). The focus then becomes the reading and writing, rather than writing as a vehicle for playing out power relations within the classroom.

A second insight that emerged has to do with the role of the teacher in writing workshops. Lensmire suggests that teacher intervention and guidance are central to the successful implementation of writing workshops. He cautions that he is not advocating "a stifling, silencing teacher control over the talk and texts of children" (p. 158). Instead, his research led him to call for a balance between absolute teacher control and complete student autonomy where children's intentions and the materials they produce are unexamined. Lensmire's research caused him to rethink, or re-vision, writing workshops as settings in which teachers and youngsters work together to make them "hospitable, supportive places for all children to write themselves and their world on the page" (p. 158).

Another revision of writing workshop suggests an expansion in the kinds of feedback middle-school children receive from peers about their writing. Farnan and Fearn (1993) used small-group sessions, which they called writers' workshops and which were modeled on the professional workshop sessions commonly held among adult practicing writers, for the purpose of giving and receiving feedback on writing. The researchers describe the outcomes of a yearlong study in a sixth-grade classroom where adolescents met weekly to share writing and receive "direct and functional feedback to support their rethinking and revising" (p. 62). Students were first provided with models of constructive feedback focused on the writing, not the writer. Their responsibility was to give useful feedback to one another regarding what made the writing work—what made it effective or what interfered with its effectiveness. After analyzing students' feedback comments throughout the year, the researchers concluded that these sixth graders tended to deliver feedback that was similar to that modeled by their teachers. Feedback comments focused on detail, clarity, and the craft of writing. Peers provided specific information that working writers could use.

There may be many new practices within process pedagogy as teachers explore children's writing and their interactions with one another. Focusing on social dynamics as a critical element in writing classrooms, Dyson (1993b) argues that we need to enlarge the lens through which we view children's social worlds within these classroom writing experiences. She proposes some questions for teacher reflection:

- With whom do children interact?
- What topics and genres do they choose, or fail to choose? What responses do they value from others or offer others?
- What links exist among children's texts and their in-school relationships and their out-of-school lives? (p. 12)

By situating children's writing within the social and cultural patterns of children's lives, more flexible views of difference and broader views of development are possible.

Critics of Writing Workshop Programs

Tobin (1994) describes the curriculum debates of the 1990s in his commentary about an emphasis on writing-process programs. He charges that "the term writing process has always been misleading" (p. 5), and that an emphasis on writing process has come to mean an

47

emphasis on process instead of product. Tobin claims that in the minds of some critics, a writing-process perspective has come to imply a nearly complete rejection of the importance of products, form, and correctness.

Such an extreme interpretation of writing process has led some detractors to see a process emphasis as simply another educational fad. Within the debate about a perceived literacy crisis in the United States, opponents of process instruction have begun to argue that it is time to get back to basics, back to standards and models of good writing. Tobin notes that even advocates for writing-process instruction have begun to criticize "the writing process movement's radical support for student writing and student freedom" (p. 6). However, the research on writing workshops, which represent an instructional environment designed to support young writers' engagement in writing process, shows an emphasis on both writing processes and product (text) development. Writers write to express ideas and present information. They write to communicate through text, and they mobilize writing processes as they seek to do this clearly and effectively. Based on research on writing workshops and conferences, several implications emerge that inform classroom instruction.

Classroom Implications and Ideas for Instruction

Recent research on writing workshops suggests the complexity of teachers' roles in helping young writers. One of the most important teaching functions is to expand choices that students have in their writing. Techniques such as minilessons and extensive genre studies introduce students to a greater range of choices and help them use a broader range of strategies in their own writing.

Another key role is to help writers cope with the difficulties of peer feedback and develop a realistic sense of how writing differs from one writing endeavor to the next. Demonstrations by the teacher of how to handle suggestions from others may help writers think about their work in relation to the comments of others. Teachers may need to model how they think through the problems that they encounter as they write. It may be helpful for teachers to examine their own writing process and to place themselves in the same kind of risky writing situations in which they place their students.

The relationship between teacher and student is particularly important during writing conferences. There is a fine line between helping a student become a better writer and taking ownership over a student's work. Teachers may want to consider how they might take a collaborative approach with students so that both teacher and student are working together toward the same goal—the improvement of the writing.

Because writing takes place in an essentially social context, this context can have a profound effect on what gets written and how students respond to it. Children who have a low social status within the classroom may particularly struggle with peer feedback. The teacher may want to monitor peer feedback and take control over which students work together in order to keep children from hurting one another.

Teachers also may want to seek other sources of feedback for students on their writing so that the teacher and the peers in that particular classroom are not the only sources of feedback about a student's writing. Especially when it is difficult to connect with a particular student's writing, finding a writing mentor from outside the classroom to provide response and information might be helpful.

Because young writers seem to respond in various ways to writing workshop and conferences, asking students to think about how they perceive the effect of those instructional processes on them as writers and on their writing may be useful. These reflections could be recorded in workshop conference logs and could inform teachers, as well as the students themselves, about how these settings are or are not contributing to their growth as writers.

Looking Ahead

Our review of writing workshop references reveals that there are far more books about how to conduct these programs than systematic studies about their effectiveness. More research is necessary to examine how children develop as writers at the primary, intermediate, and middle grades in these programs. We need to know what supports children's learning and how they make sense of process-oriented writing instruction. The bulk of existing research looks at first graders and beginning writing instruction. New research about intermediate-grade and middle-school children in process-oriented writing programs needs to include studies that focus on what writers grapple with at these grade levels and what supports writing growth. As writing workshops increasingly focus on in-depth genre studies, research needs to analyze children's growing understandings of different genres. We need descriptions of successful writing workshops in the intermediate and upper grades and detailed documentation of effective ways for working with children who are outsiders in the peer culture. And finally, we need descriptions from teachers about what supports their continuing development as they refine process-writing programs at various grade levels.

CHAPTER 4

Learning the Craft of Writing

We purposefully used the word "craft" in the title of this chapter because writing requires skill, expertise, and the use of many strategies that will help the writer draft (or "craft") a clear, coherent, and effective composition. Some of these elements and strategies are more global in nature, relating broadly to the composing of a text, such as the shaping of a piece of writing for a particular audience. Some, such as the writer using planning and revision strategies, require stepping back from a text (or potential text) and taking a critical look. And some involve developing knowledge about conventional surface features of texts, such as spelling and punctuation. In this chapter we focus on these and other elements that are critical to the craft of writing. We discuss how children learn a variety of strategies such as developing audience awareness and learning to use the conventions of writing as they write in the company of other writers in school.

Audience Awareness

Interest in audience awareness stems from a conviction that writers use their vision of an intended audience to make decisions that shape a writing. A sense of audience can help young writers figure out what to include, what to leave out, and how to present their ideas. Audience awareness also drives some of the decisions that writers make as they revise.

Perhaps the most well-known investigation of audience was conducted by Britton, Burgess, Martin, McLeod, and Rosen (1975). In this classic study, more than 2,000 pieces of school writing by students aged 11 to 18 were rated as being in one of the following audience categories: self, teacher, wider audience (known), and unknown audience. The expectation was that older students would write for more differentiated and distant audiences and for more distant ones. The ratings, however, at all levels showed that most of the writing (between 87% and 99%) was written to the teacher as audience. Although this finding might have been expected (all the pieces were school writing), the instructional intent in the classrooms was that young writers across the grades were learning to write for the purpose of communicating with various audiences.

Some of the other studies on audience have looked at writers from various grade levels and tried to gather developmental data about when writers differentiate their writing for varying audiences. The developmental picture usually shows that children in the elementary grades are not particularly aware of audience in comparison with children in the upper grades. For example, when Langer (1986) asked children in Grades 3, 6, and 9 to answer questions about their writing and talk about audience, the elementary-grade children demonstrated tacit understanding of author-audience relationships; they seemed to understand that their role as authors was to communicate meaning and could talk about how they met the needs of particular audiences. However, they were not interested in examining these strategies. The younger writers (Grade 3) were more concerned with neatness and achieving enough length to their reports than they were with the details of the language they selected. Older writers seemed to show an awareness of and concern for audience, as they were interested in determining whether a particular report would be boring or too difficult for their readers. They did not, however, talk about concerns for audience as a general feature of their writing.

More recently, an investigation by Frank (1992) addressed how well fifth-grade writers could revise an informational piece of writing to communicate with two differing audiences, a third-grade reader and an adult. The idea of this research was to select a realistic task (writing an advertisement) in which the audience could evaluate the effectiveness of the writer's communication. This study showed that fifth graders were able to target the two audience groups with some success and write appropriately for each. The author suggests that elementary students need opportunities to address real audiences outside their own classrooms so they may learn to communicate effectively.

Frank's study is in sharp contrast to a developmental study by Kroll (1985) in which writers in Grades 5, 7, 9, and 11 and college freshmen adapted a linguistically complex story, rewriting it for a third-grade reader. The fifth graders in Kroll's study were more word oriented in their rewriting for the young audience than were their older counterparts. The fifth graders made revisions by replacing difficult words with simpler ones; their revisions were made on a word-for-word basis. Older writers, on the other hand, used meaning-oriented strategies by generally rewriting the story, but preserving the meaning and structure.

These studies of children's sense of audience largely reflect the Piagetian notion that young children's writing tends to be egocentric, directed toward satisfying the self rather than others. This view is challenged, however, in Dyson's research (1994) in which she describes children performing their written works in author's theater formats. When primary-grade children tried their writing by having others use it as a script, they saw what their audience needed and how that audience responded to written ideas. It therefore appears that certain instructional processes, such as author's theater experiences, may help young writers think about their audience as they sort out ways to tell their stories.

Planning

Understanding how writers plan is critical to figuring out how to help students become effective writers, yet this kind of information is not easy to "get at" because often planning is a silent, thoughtful activity. Bereiter and Scardamalia (1987) conducted research designed to make the mental processes more obvious, asking writers to plan their writing before drafting. Participants were encouraged to take notes but not actually write the text. The differences between novices and more expert writers were noticeable.

Younger, novice writers tended to create notes that were later transcribed directly as the text of their writing. This composing behavior tended to persist until writers were in early adolescence (approximately age 12). More experienced writers, however, tended to transform their notes, which included such things as organizational arrows and signals, lists, and groupings of related ideas, into a text that may have contained some of the ideas but that maintained no resemblance to the original notetaking. When asked to plan, the young adults seemed to work through a writing task at a more global, abstract level before committing the ideas to the more linear and concrete form of text. For younger, novice writers, on the other hand, planning seemed to occur at the same level of thinking as the actual writing of the text. It appears that the activity itself, the cue to plan before doing the actual writing, did not alter the processes used by the younger writers. Maturity thus seems to be a significant factor in whether writers are able to separate their plans for writing from the actual text itself.

Bereiter and Scardamalia (1987) attempted to provide planning strategies that would separate children's planning from their actual text writing. The researchers' objective was to force children away from the "think-write-think-write pattern" (p. 197), thereby giving them opportunities to distance the planning from the actual text writing. Interestingly, when they told children that adults sometimes take 15 minutes or longer to plan before writing, the children were astonished. "They could not imagine what there was to think about for that length of time" (p. 197). This research involved students in Grades 4, 6, and 8, who were asked to think aloud and plan for as long as they could before writing. They were encouraged to think about such things as the difficulties they might encounter in a writing, what they already knew related to the topic, what their goals were for the writing, how someone reading their text might react to it, and how they might put all of these ideas together to create a "really good paragraph." Students in a control group were given these same topics around which to plan, but they were merely given them on cards and were told that if they had difficulty with the writing, they might want to use the cards.

The findings were consistent with data from other studies. Through early adolescence, even in the experimental group in which children were engaged in actively planning before writing, children did not seem to be able to separate their planning from their text writing; their plans simply became the texts. As students became older, their planning notes began to look quite different from the texts they wrote, both in form and in content. It appears, from these and other studies that make up a fairly extensive body of research, that maturity is a rather significant factor in writers' ability to move beyond focusing all of their attention on producing the immediate text, and instead to begin planning and crafting a text around consideration of such things as objectives for a writing; the writer's knowledge of content, discourse structures, and text organization; and problem-solving strategies.

There is, however, a qualifier to these findings. Bereiter and Scardamalia (1987) report anecdotal evidence from school situations in which the social interactions of conferences, peer discussions, and cooperative writing occur. There they found evidence that group interactions can promote a higher level of planning, even in very young children. The researchers found that when a variety of alternative ideas were presented in a collaborative setting, children were forced to weigh and analyze ideas before writing. In these cases, planning was much more conceptual and did not represent simply a mirror image of the composition itself.

Children's Understanding of Genres

Children show that they can use a variety of genres in their early writing in school. As early as first grade, children write lists, labels, and signs, as well as rudimentary narratives. Their drawings often seem to include the addition of written captions. They also explore the variety of print available in their classroom environments. For example, they copy the words on displays, story charts, and bulletin boards. Although it may seem logical that narratives would be the prevalent genre in the early grades, current research indicates that children use both expository and narrative genres at the primary level.

Chapman's (1995) investigation of genres was situated in a classroom writing program and traces the genres appearing in children's writing across the span of a school year. In this study, genres are defined as forms or ways of organizing and structuring discourse that are shaped by their use or the context in which they occur.

As would be expected, the genres demonstrated in the classroom by the first-grade teacher also were used by children in their own writing. For instance, the word plays, songs, and poems used by the teacher were reworked into new versions. Children also generated narratives that were action-event oriented writings drawn from experience or from imagination. These included chronologies of events with various levels of related or unrelated information.

Children also produced writings in which the focus was on objects rather than events. These writings had logical relations rather than chronological ones, and included lists, labels, attribute series (I like dogs, I like cats, I like birds), verse, and word plays in which children played with language as an object. Some of the word plays were playful drawings with words or letters included, others were original versions of familiar verses. Finally, children generated writing for social action in the form of notes or written dialogues.

Chapman presents this array of classroom genres as sociocognitive constructions because they capture both social and cognitive processes influencing children's writing. In her study children appropriated various genres from classroom experiences, such as stories, morning news, and classroom poems. They also acted on their classroom environment using writing to tell about experiences and experiment with written language. We note that both narrative and expository forms were developing in this classroom across various categories.

In addition to the Chapman study, other research documenting various genres has focused on the development of expository writing. Newkirk (1987) analyzed the non-narrative forms of writing appearing in first, second, and third graders' portfolios. He found a range of expository texts with complex forms (that is, paragraph, attribute series) to be more prevalent in the third-grade samples, although the first graders' expository writing was predominately list and label, with some linked sentences (couplets) and unordered paragraphs. Although Newkirk's categorization of various types of expository writing was not designed specifically to document developmental patterns, his analysis did demonstrate two main findings: that expository forms evident in first grade (list and label) were not forms used as frequently by third graders, and that these first-grade efforts were related to the sorting and display of information. Newkirk argues that "exposition may well begin not as speech written down, but as the appropriation and extension of dominant literate forms—the list and the label" (p. 141).

The writing-reading research by Langer (1986) provides developmental descriptions about children's knowledge of story and report genres. This analysis shows that children approach these genres in different ways across the grades and show a developmental gap between their facility with stories and with reports. For third graders, story structures in writing are already in place, with time orderings often governing the overall story structures that children use. In contrast, children's ways of structuring reports change radically among third, sixth, and ninth grade. At third grade, children's reports show a simple thesis and elaboration structure, such as listing. At sixth and ninth grade, the gap between story structure knowledge and report knowledge narrows and children show increasing control of structures that allow linking and elaboration of information to produce more complex, coherent reports.

There is growth between the ages of 11 and 14 in children's overall organizational facility with reports. They are able to embed multiple pieces of information, to elaborate, and to improve the organization of their reports. The structures of ninth graders' reports, however, do not seem to include the more complex forms needed to structure and support an argument (cause and effect or problem and solution). It appears that young writers begin at an early age to craft writings across a variety of genres. Factors that seem to influence their genre writing include purpose and social context, as well as reading experiences and maturation.

Revision

Many instructional issues are raised about revision. Revision may be the key to learning the craft of writing, not only a critical dimension for producing improved final drafts but also a vehicle for gaining process understanding. Revision encompasses not only the changes after the pen hits the paper, but also the in-the-head changes as writers think about their texts.

Children's revisions include everything from simple surface structure moves (such as erasing, adding punctuation, and crossing out unneeded words) to rethinking the fundamental focus or point-of-view of a story. Revision occurs in any subprocess of children's composing and is related to the intentions and expertise of the writer. In our view, the critical information about revision involves three issues:

1. understanding the influences of age and expertise on children's revisions so that reasonable revision information can be demonstrated, talked about, and supported in classroom writing programs;
2. determining whether there are support systems or writing experiences that can successfully prompt revisions; and
3. figuring out the young writer's perspective on revising in relation to the writing event or problem of the moment.

The body of research on children's revisions is, to a great extent, about writing with paper and pencil, though we will report some computer-centered revision research. We have yet to experience a generation of elementary- and middle-school children who have written primarily on computers and who are adept at computer strategies for generating and moving text, deleting, merging drafts, and printing out alternative versions. This generation of school writers will likely show us new dimensions of revision and may require new kinds of instructional support.

Research shows that some primary-grade children begin to revise as soon as they begin to write. They cross out or erase words in the midst of drafting; they add new words as they draft, reread, and continue drafting; and they add more text at the end of their pieces. (See Fitzgerald, 1987, for a comprehensive review of revision research.)

The relation between children's egocentricity and the kinds of revisions demonstrated by beginning writers has been supported in research. Generally, beginning writers do not carry out substantial revisions, though they do engage in a greater number of revisions when someone else points out what could be revised. They also are more adept at detecting the need for revision in the writing of others than in their own work.

Some beginning writers see writing as fixed and nonnegotiable. For these young writers and for those primary-grade writers who physically struggle with the task of producing letters and words, there may be substantial resistance to revision. These writers like their writing "the way it is" and think revision is mostly about copying the entire piece over, a prospect that holds little attraction from their perspective.

Calkins's Research on Revision

Studies that look closely at children writing over time are of particular interest as we consider the effects of age and expertise on children's revisions. We turn now to the seminal work of Lucy Calkins as reported in *Lessons From a Child* (1983) and summarize the findings from that work related to revision.

In her work, Calkins closely follows the writing development of one learner, tracing her writing growth across third and fourth grades. Calkins notes that instruction from minilessons, individual conferences, sustained writing activity, and demonstrations substantially enhance revision activity for this learner.

More complex revisions in fourth grade occur as procedures (such as writing several leads in order to have alternative ways of beginning a piece) are talked about in the classroom. Revisions also become more complex as the writer experiments with and gains facility with alternative drafts.

Some revision benchmarks within Calkins's case study include the young writer experimenting with the following:

- Writing a series of leads as options for a piece.
- Thinking through alternative leads as an internalized process.
- Moving from past drafts of a story to a new future version of the story that anticipates an audience.
- Identifying parts of an initial draft to expand with details in a subsequent draft (circle and expand).
- Considering options or alternative directions for a draft.
- Evaluating how the pieces of a draft fit together.
- Eliminating whole sections from a piece.
- Using a dividing-line strategy for eliminating story sections. This strategy marked text to be deleted by drawing a dividing line between it and the text to be retained.
- Developing an alternative version of a piece.

Generally, as this young writer grew in sophistication, the distinctions between revising and composing blurred, and the writer moved into increasingly complex ways of thinking about writing.

Procedural Support for Revision

Other studies addressing revision have investigated the need for procedural support. Some researchers contend that children in the intermediate grades may have difficulty knowing how to make revisions and may experience problems with the executive control necessary to manage the entire process. A line of research by Bereiter and Scardamalia (1987), in which they taught children in Grades 4, 6, and 8 specific revision routines, suggests that children are able to learn how to use executive routines for evaluation and revision of their writing. For example, this research indicates that children who are taught a specific text-analysis procedure (compare, diagnose, and choose) use that procedure effectively during composing. *Compare* in this procedure means that young writers think about the intended meaning and compare that with what they have actually written. *Diagnose* means the writer examines the text and uses his rhetorical knowledge to discover the cause of the mismatch (for example, by asking, Is the idea clear? Is there enough information?). *Choose* means selecting a tactic (such as changing a wording or adding or deleting an item) in order to act on the difficulty. Children move from a view of revision as merely "thinking of something different or more to say" (p. 296) to pinpointing specifically what could be changed in their writing.

Additional research by Fitzgerald and Markham (1987) documenting this revision intervention with sixth-grade writers finds that young writers can develop an enhanced ability to identify discrepancies between their goals and intentions for a piece. They also demonstrate an increase in their knowledge of what to change and how to make desired changes when they use these procedures.

Research about revision and procedural knowledge also includes computer programs designed to prompt writers about specific revisions. Computer programs provide lists of text features that writers can consider (such as completeness, clarity, organization, coherence, sentence structure, and punctuation). After each segment of text, either a single sentence or group of sentences, the computer program presents options phrased as questions to guide the writer's thinking. For example, one prompt might ask the writer to examine the introduction of a report: Is the topic of the report stated clearly? These programs offer support for self-questioning and are designed to help writers identify which text features to examine more closely. The results of research by Daiute (1986) show that writers composing on computers without revision-prompting programs tend, when revising, to move to the end of their texts and simply add a section. They engage in increased editing activity on the computer but make fewer global text revisions than their counterparts who work with revision-prompting programs. This study suggests that prompts may help relatively inexperienced writers focus on various kinds of possible revisions. (See Chapter 6 for discussion on issues of writing and computers.)

A reference for teachers focused on revision instruction and the revision problems that children experience is *After the End: Teaching and Learning Creative Revision* (Lane, 1993). This work presents lessons showing revision strategies and specific suggestions for instruction, and describes spin-offs for key points that can stimulate teaching ideas.

Spelling and Punctuation

Adequate spelling growth and understanding of punctuation are two of the expected outcomes of writing workshop programs. Although explicit instruction on the conventions of writing (for example, spelling, punctuation, and capitalization) may not be the central focus in classrooms that emphasize writing processes, many classroom writing programs address these issues in editing sessions and instructional minilessons.

The body of research on spelling development documents how children's spelling progresses from early symbolic and phonetic strategies to more complex approaches using various kinds of oral and written language information. (For comprehensive descriptions of these early developmental patterns, see Beers & Henderson, 1977, or Gentry & Gillet, 1993; Treiman [1993, pp. 25–38] also provides an extended historical review of research that describes the work of various groups of researchers over the past few decades.)

Although the majority of spelling research focuses on early spelling development, spelling-reading connections, or spelling assessment, the primary interest in this chapter is research that connects spelling to the actual writing program. We spotlight three studies that explore important issues.

Treiman's Qualitative Spelling Research

A qualitative study by Treiman (1993) tracks first graders learning to spell and analyzes the mistakes they make at the beginning and end of the school year. The children were in a classroom encouraging invented spelling and were told to figure out words the best they could. The study's findings indicate that these first graders at year's end

- often spelled correctly words that they had seen frequently;
- produced spellings that were attempts to represent sounds;
- attempted words that were difficult to spell;
- did not avoid function words (*and*, *the*, *of*);
- struggled with long words, irregular words, and inflected words; and
- had difficulty with words with adjacent clusters of consonants (plant) and words where phonemes were represented by more than one letter (thin).

Treiman argues that, for these young writers, spelling is a process drawing sometimes on visual memory and sometimes also on phonemic understanding. She describes the value of children's writing experiences in early spelling growth:

> Writing requires children to think about the sounds and meanings of spoken words, to observe the characteristics of printed words, and to form hypotheses about the relations between sounds and letters. All of these activities are of great value in helping children grasp the alphabetic nature of the English writing system. (p. 289)

An important feature of this investigation is its comprehensive portrayal of the varying spelling strategies used by first graders and the researcher's detailed description of each finding in relation to other perspectives on spelling research.

Comparative Spelling Research

The second study compares spelling progress for first-grade children in two contrasting conditions with respect to instructions about spelling within the writing period. Two classrooms were encouraged to use invented spellings in their writing, and two classrooms that were matched in terms of socioeconomic status with the other participants were encouraged to use traditional spellings (Clarke, 1988). Each of the four classrooms used the same basal reading program and taught phonics in similar ways in connection to the language arts program. The study analyzed children's spelling strategies during writing sessions, and also compared their spelling performance in writing samples over a 5-month period and on posttests of spelling and reading achievement.

The findings showed that children using invented spelling spent their time writing unaided from recall, sounding out the words and listening to the teacher talk to them or to other children. In contrast, traditional spellers used information from references such as dictionaries, personal word lists, or wall charts and asked the teacher for help. The analysis of writing samples showed that the traditional spellers had a significantly higher percentage of words above the first-grade level spelled correctly, although the invented spellers were higher in the increased numbers of invented spellings at Gentry's Transitional and Phonetic Stages across the five-month period. Transitional spellings include visual strategies to spell words. They are an attempt to write the sounds and to make a word look like a word in English. These spellings often use vowels in every syllable and have most of the letters in a conventional spelling, though not in the correct order. Phonetic spellings, in contrast, focus on sound. Children systematically represent the sounds they hear in a word.

The two groups did not differ much in the number of different words they attempted, though the compositions from the invented spellers were significantly longer. Although the students experienced the same reading program, the various posttest results revealed that the invented spellers had higher achievement on word-analysis tasks (including spelling achievement), and the traditional spellers were higher on word recognition with flashcards. When these scores were compared by high and low achievers, the high achievers in both groups scored about the same. The groups differed in the low groups; low achievers using invented spelling had significantly higher scores on six of the posttest reading tasks. Clarke explains the unexpected difference in the area of phonic analysis:

> The superior spelling and phonic analysis skill of children using invented spelling suggested that they benefited from the practice of matching

sound segments of words to letters as they wrote and from using their own sound sequence analysis. These differences were major considering that both groups were using basal readers which promote a reliance on processing words by their visual cues rather than by phonic analysis. (p. 307)

This study seemed to offer evidence that, over a 5-month period, the traditional spellers were more successful in using traditional spellings in their writing and the invented spellers seemed to gather insights about phonic analysis as they grappled with spelling intended words.

Both this study and the previous one suggest the value of encouraging invented spellings in first grade and document that children learn some spelling concepts through writing. They also show us that children experiencing traditional spelling are successfully able to use the resources in the room and do spell conventionally with such supports.

Case Study Spelling Research

The third spelling study investigates the spelling development of third- and fourth-grade Native American children. It was conducted through analysis of samples from classroom writing and included case studies of children's spelling processes (Wilde, 1988). In general, children in this sample spelled frequently used words conventionally and generated nonconventional spellings for words used infrequently, struggling with features that were less predictable. Their spellings indicated that initial letters, digraphs, and vowels were usually spelled conventionally. As expected, analyses showed considerable spelling development between third and fourth grade with statistically significant changes, for example, in children's control of -ed suffixes and less predictable vowels. Many misspellings were real words or permutations of intended words, and some invented spellings seemed to reflect use of phonetic knowledge. Interestingly, there were marked differences in individual speller's hypotheses about spelling and strategies for spelling unknown words. Some children wrote EAT for *ate* (using a digraph spelling for the vowel rather than the conventional silent final E), and another wrote DILFTSCT for *breakfast*, a spelling that violated expected spelling patterns and strategies.

This study is important in its documentation of continued spelling growth and its description of individual spelling processes. It indicates that as students bring new words into their writing they grapple with additional aspects of orthography. It also suggests that differences across learners may be more striking than the developmental progression in spelling that has received so much research attention.

Spelling resources

The work on spelling also includes a number of books describing classroom spelling or word-study programs that could be integrated with process-centered writing curricula. One book, *Words Their Way: Word Study for Phonics, Vocabulary, and Spelling Instruction* (Bear, Invernizzi, Templeton, & Johnston, 1996), provides not only background information about the development of orthographic knowledge, but detailed information about word-study principles and lessons for primary- and intermediate-grade children. These lessons include elementary spelling inventories for assessment (p. 38) and listings of activities matched for sequences of development (word banks, picture sorts for beginnings and ends of words, and word-study notebooks). Another text, *You Kan Red This!* (Wilde, 1992), presents minilessons on spelling for writing workshop programs, as well as information for developing grade-level spelling programs and descriptions of spelling strategies to teach children. Minilessons include strategies for trying spellings and information regarding specific spelling patterns (plural endings with *-es*, past tense words, and preconsonantal nasals, for example, *n* in *song*).

Teachers expanding spelling instruction within the writing program may want to align specific word-study lessons with spelling patterns from children's writing. In an article combining theory, research, and teaching suggestions, Invernizzi, Abouzeid, and Gill (1994) present an array of spelling minilessons that address children's invented spelling patterns. For example, for learners who are experimenting with sounds and spelling, they describe the following minilessons:

> *Picture sorting*—a categorization task in which students group items with similar features in terms of sound (rhyme or initial consonant sounds).
>
> *Word sorting*—categorizing words by similar features in guided lessons and then independent work.

65

Word hunting—searching with teacher guidance in existing writing for words that have specific patterns and listing them.

For learners who are more advanced and are working with word patterns, activities can focus on both sound and pattern. Word sorts and word hunts, for example, may focus on inflectional endings of words or on finding and categorizing words ending in *y*. Finally, learners who are experimenting with meaning relations and spelling can explore word derivations and word patterns involving prefixes, suffixes, and root words. These minilesson activities engage children in examining and manipulating words and their spellings.

Learning About Punctuation

The amount of research on punctuation learning is far smaller than the body of work on children's spelling. Research by Cordiero, Giacobbe, and Cazden (1983) documents first graders' developing concepts of possessive apostrophes, quotation marks, and periods in a first-grade writing workshop program. In this study, children's vigorous exploration of punctuation reflects their interest in and frequent attempts to use these marks, for example, using periods after every word or at the end of each line, adding apostrophes to plurals or verbs, and using these punctuation marks correctly. The authors found that periods were the most difficult to teach first graders because children held alternative hypotheses about when to use periods. Students were confused by sentence construction and their use of periods in one piece of writing was followed by periods in the wrong place or omission of the period in the next piece. Explanations to first graders that periods belong where the voice stops or falls were ineffective, leading sometimes to phrase divisions being marked with periods. Cordiero (1988) extended this analysis by comparing first graders' uses of periods to her third graders' developing understanding. Her comparison showed development of textual punctuation, but also indicated that as the sentences grew more complex, students encountered new difficulties.

Wilde (1996) also looked at punctuation efforts in writing samples of third and fourth graders. She found that periods constituted 87% of the punctuation used and that in about two thirds of the attempts, periods were used successfully. Commas and quotation marks seemed to cause the most difficulty at these grade levels. The results, presented with descriptions of each of the six learners as they progressed across the 2-year span of the study, showed that knowledge of punctuation differed widely among these learners. Wilde also found that growth in punctuation knowledge can develop when students' experimentation in writing was accompanied by individual feedback and instruction. Children in the Wilde investigation first focused attention on periods and then experimented with other marks, coming to an understanding of quotation marks last.

A review of research about punctuation presents an insufficient picture of children learning the functions and meanings of punctuation. Research does not provide descriptions of the sense that children make of punctuation within the context of their writing. Hall & Robinson (1996) summarize existing studies and include some current classroom investigations with various grade levels and populations. This reference is an encouraging development, inviting increased inquiry into writing and punctuation. In its introductory chapter, Nigel Hall (1996) poses questions for the field, suggesting directions for classroom research into the following:

- the development of knowledge about punctuation over extended periods of time.

- the relations between classroom experiences and learning about punctuation, exploring the kinds of conditions that are effective in encouraging the most efficient learning about punctuation.

- whether experience of different kinds of texts has any influence on children's use and knowledge of punctuation. (p. 35)

Classroom Implications and Ideas for Instruction

Writing occurs at a critical point in children's cognitive development. In Piagetian terms, children between the ages of 6 to 14 go through developmental processes in which they shed the egocentrism with which they are born. As children progress from the early stages of development, they begin to understand that other people's perspectives exist, and they learn to imagine those other perspectives. Because writing is a form of communication, it offers ideal occasions for children to have the cognitively dissonant experiences that help them to progress in this direction.

A crucial element in this process is audience. Students need to have a variety of real audiences for their writing if they are to learn to adapt their work to the needs of a variety of readers. Teachers can find real audiences within the classroom, within the school, within students' families, within the larger community, and, with the advent of the Internet, across the world. For example, older students can be encouraged to write children's books for younger students. Children also can exchange letters with numerous pen pals—other children in the same city or town, older people who share their interest in a particular topic, or classrooms of learners studying the same subject matter on the other side of the globe.

Planning is probably the aspect of writing most influenced by development. Young children cannot even imagine what adults would think about in a lengthy planning session. Yet, because collaborative texts require negotiation among writers at the beginning of and throughout a writing, even young children must engage in extensive planning when collaborating. Teachers may wish to encourage collaborative writing for young students (and even for older students) and then help students explicitly connect the planning strategies they use in groups with strategies they might use when writing alone.

Revision is another important element as writers craft a text and yet very young children are likely to resist revision, particularly if they see it simply as copying a piece. Writers benefit from prompts about revising—a series of questions for the writer to consider both during and after writing. The teacher might want to generate these questions with students and demonstrate the process of considering these questions in relation to a piece of writing. As the school year progresses, the class can add to the questions they consider. Teachers can also demonstrate how computer use helps the revision process (by facilitating the movement of text, allowing for easy substitution of words or sections, and providing spell checking).

Writing involves both visual and aural strategies. Teachers can remind children as they write to think about words they have seen as well as sounding out words as they are written. Invented spelling can help readers learn about how language works. It does not hold back able writers. Numerous helpful activities that support spelling growth and punctuation learning exist and can be incorporated into the writing program both through minilessons and in individual and small-group conferences.

Looking Ahead

The research we have presented on children's expertise as writers, specifically their knowledge of audience, genre, revising, and use of conventions reveals some developmental trends as children gain control of particular writing skills. More needs to be done to discover the effects of audience awareness on students across age levels and as they write in various genres. It appears that there are developmental issues associated with this ability. It would be useful to know how young writers perceive the role that audience awareness has in their writing. Do some children, as some practicing and experienced writers report, find that their own purposes for writing are more powerful than their attention to audience? Or do young writers report that awareness of audience helps them in their writing? If so, it would be important to know in what ways. Also, would it vary according to the type of writing?

The studies of writing in various genres provide a beginning for our understanding of children's writing. This research does not provide a sufficient developmental picture, nor does it provide information about how children learn the structures of various genres across the grades. We need to know how to support children's developing understandings of the various genres in writing, and we need to examine the social and cognitive factors that influence children's writing across the genres.

Research has begun to tap into the cognitive aspects of children's revisions. We have begun to document the knowledge sources and experiences that help children see a need to revise their writings. We have some general information about the development across grade levels of children's ability to revise. The list of research that is needed, however, is an extensive one. Will children who are taught specific revision routines actually use them when working independently? What supports for revision are most productive for learners at various grade levels? What revision strategies do children use most when they recopy their works manually and make scattered revisions?

There is still much to be learned about spelling and use of other conventions associated with writing, such as punctuation and capitalization. What processes and strategies best support students as they use invented or temporary spellings in their writings to learn about language and, at the same time, help students move smoothly into traditional or conventional spelling in their writing? Given the value of temporary spellings to help children explore and learn about language, and given the value of learning conventional spelling, it is important to discover what strategies or combinations of strategies seem best to support both objectives. Yet another question relates to *what* teachers should teach, that is, the content of instruction in spelling (for example, naked word lists, words in categories, words from writing and literature, pattern study, structural analysis, and so forth) in order to support students' growth in their spelling ability.

Regarding the use of punctuation, it appears, again, that young writers experiment with the use of commas, periods, and apostrophes, but that children's understandings of their appropriate use are often unclear. In addition, as their understandings develop, their writings also become more complex and the punctuation conventions become more difficult. A fundamental question centers on how to best teach punctuation (what instructional processes and strategies) so that students become even more effective users of the conventions in their writing. What conventions should be taught and when, in order to best support youngsters in their development as effective writers? Is young writers' confusion about the use of conventions related to their understandings of how sentences are constructed? If so, how can teachers best help children develop a "sense of sentence"? What reading-related experiences support these understandings?

These areas of study can inform classroom practice, providing documentation for teachers who are concerned about children's compositions and who are interested in ways to help young writers become more proficient in the craft of writing.

CHAPTER 5

Writing Across Subject Areas

The role of writing in children's learning across various content areas and how the connections among writing, thinking, and reading can be used to support learning are important considerations for teachers. Researchers have asked a number of questions about writing and other subject areas: What are the relations between writing and thinking? How do children write about information? What are the connections between writing and mathematics? How are writing and reading connected for learners?

This chapter looks at research on writing as it occurs in various subject areas. The research is organized around two broad sets of relations: the connections between thinking and writing as children write across the curriculum and the connections between reading and writing in various subject areas. We look specifically at research on instructional practices that integrate writing into the areas of mathematics, social studies, and literature.

Writing and Thinking Connections

Because writing processes are closely tied to cognitive processes, a natural link exists between writing and thinking. Writing across the curriculum for the purpose of strengthening learning carries the assumption that, somehow, the processes of writing will lead to better understandings of ideas and concepts, many of which students encounter in their readings across content areas.

In their 1987 research on the role of writing in thinking, Langer and Applebee conceptualize this relation in the following ways:

- Writing is permanent and allows the writer to "rethink and revise over an extended period" (p. 5).

- Writing requires the writer to construct meaning explicitly by taking meaning beyond its original form (that is, text, discussion, or lecture).

- Writing causes the writer to think through relations among ideas.

- The constructive, active nature of writing provides an opportunity for exploring ideas and assumptions that might otherwise go unexamined.

Within this framework Langer and Applebee posed several fundamental questions about the role of writing in students' learning: What are the effects of writing in a variety of academic settings? Do some writing tasks have more effect than others on learning? Does writing have a purpose beyond its use as an assessment process? Should writing be integrated throughout the curriculum for purposes of enhancing thinking and learning?

The secondary-level teachers collaborating with Langer and Applebee were 23 science, home economics, English, and social studies teachers who were interested in incorporating more writing into their classrooms. After working 3 years with these teachers and their students, the researchers concluded that writing does assist learning, but that not all writing is equal in its effect on learning. Instead, they found that "different kinds of writing activities lead students to focus on different kinds of information, to think about that information in different ways, and...to take different kinds of knowledge away from their writing experiences" (p. 135). For example, the researchers concluded that short-answer study questions lead only to short-term recall of information and that little rethinking and reflection about the text and its ideas take place. These kinds of activities require students only to find information in text and copy it onto a study sheet. In this process they tend to pick out specific information, with little emphasis on relations among ideas, and simply transcribe it onto their paper. The resulting effect on their learning is not surprising.

In contrast, other writing tasks cause students to manipulate the ideas in the text. In these instances, students may not capture as much information, but they seem to capture it in more depth. And, although some information may not be as accessible to short-term recall, memory for ideas tends to be longer lived and students tend to remember relations among ideas and information and to have more complex understandings of the ideas. These kinds of writing tasks are more analytic than other writing tasks such as notetaking and summary writing. In analytic writing, students are asked to do such things as compare and contrast, evaluate, explain, and draw conclusions. In other words, students are not asked simply to restate information and ideas, but to think about them.

Langer and Applebee also discovered that it is critical for students to understand the point of a task and for teachers and students to have a shared understanding of the specific goals of an instructional event. They describe five components of instructional scaffolding in relation to writing tasks across subject areas:

1. Ownership: Students must have a sense that the task has value for them, and they must know what that value is.

2. Support: Students must understand how a given writing task supports what they are learning.

3. Appropriateness: The writing tasks must be ones that students have the knowledge and skill to complete.

4. Collaborative: A collaborative role for the teacher supports the writing-learning connection through acts such as modeling, questioning, and providing feedback. The role of the writing teacher is more collaborative than evaluative.

5. Internalization: Students must internalize the strategies available to them for writing to learn, and they must come to see writing as a natural part of the thinking and learning processes.

Overall, Langer and Applebee's research led them to the conclusion that writing in content areas is useful in three specific areas: (1) to gain necessary knowledge and experience for an upcoming task, such as reading a text; (2) to capture and review what has been read and learned; and (3) to reflect on, elaborate on, and extend ideas and experiences. Of these three areas, the researchers concluded that the third led to the most complex understandings and reasoning, and the second led to the least. "Think" papers—short explanations showing student ideas and reasoning—were used by some teachers in the study to begin the shift from using writing solely as a way to evaluate student work to encouraging its use for thinking.

Although this study was conducted with older learners, we think its findings raise interesting possibilities for elementary- and middle-school content-area writing instruction. Writing-thinking tasks can be appropriate for children because they provide opportunities for elaborating on ideas and reflecting on experiences. The criteria for scaffolding instructional events in content areas (ownership, support, appropriateness of activity, collaborative role for the teacher, and internalization) can be used productively for writing projects and activities to support the learning of younger students.

Writing-Thinking Research in Thematic Units

When children do projects that involve their independent explorations in subject areas (for example, in thematic studies or extended topical units), how do writing-thinking relations come into play? The research on writing has begun to explore what happens when children write to learn in various subject areas. In this section, we describe studies in which children write in their subject areas using various sources.

We have selected three studies as a sample to demonstrate how writing-thinking connections play out in children's writing. Two of the studies address what children do when they write from a variety of source materials about a topic. The first of these is a study by Many, Fyfe, Lewis, and Mitchell (1996) looking at children's reading and writing engagements in writing projects in which they produce reports. This research describes how children think about their work when they write from sources. The second, by Spivey and King (1989), looks at what children produce. It describes the composing outcomes of sixth, eighth, and tenth graders as they write from sources. The third study reveals the relation between the teacher's actions in structuring content-area projects and children's writing-thinking activities (Harper, 1997). Harper investigated children's actions during their production of writing projects in social studies, language arts, and science.

How Children Think as They Write From Sources

The Many et al. study (1996) took place as 11- and 12-year-olds in Aberdeen, Scotland, worked on a thematic unit about World War II.

The objective was to "search for and to select [information] from source materials, and to write up and present their findings in their own way" (p. 13). Learners worked from a wide variety of materials (both print and nonprint) to develop extended writing in research booklets.

The researchers observed children at work, interviewed them at various points in the development of their projects to get their perspectives, and analyzed the writing they produced. Critical to the study was understanding what children thought they were supposed to do. Those who saw their work in this project as *accumulating information* went about writing and reading in a linear way. They gathered interesting material, often turning to random discoveries without an overriding plan, and adjusted their planning webs after the fact to include each additional find. The writing strategy for this work was often search, then copy verbatim.

Learners who interpreted the task as *transferring information* engaged in either sentence-by-sentence reworking (read and then restate the text in one's own words), or they worked using a strategy of read, remember, and write. Both ways of writing and reading were confined to one text at a time and both drew on the structure and organization of the original reference. These children seemed to believe that multiple sources were important, but they strung them together piece-by-piece in order to produce their research.

A third group believed that the task was *transforming information.* This group engaged in extended and continuous planning as they searched for materials focusing on their intended direction, and they revised these plans as new possibilities emerged. Their planning process also included monitoring whether coverage of each subtopic was adequate and using multiple sources to bolster topical areas. Their writing strategies included cut-and-paste synthesis, in which they internalized information from each source and wrote about it, then constructed the separate pieces into a whole. Another strategy was closer to traditional discourse synthesis; students wrote their new texts after a process involving selecting, organizing, and connecting content. Learners were able to cross check the accuracy of their information by working across multiple sources. They maintained an awareness of audience as they made decisions about their writing.

The research team found that some learners changed their mind about what the task was and turned to new strategies. Children also were able to switch strategies as the level of difficulty in their resources changed and as the amount of time remaining diminished. Some students believed that the task was to fill completely the 15 to 20 empty pages of the research booklets. Toward the end of the project, a few children resorted to copying verbatim, while others, who were working by restating sources sentence by sentence, began synthesizing information in their own words. In addition to their task interpretations, the factors that seemed to influence children as they worked included the following:

- their own characteristics and strategies as writers and readers,
- the nature of the texts with which they were working, and
- the context in which they functioned, including time allowed to work on the project and the social dynamics of the classroom.

In reflecting on their findings, the researchers observed that children may have engaged in planning too early, that is before they knew enough about their topic. For these students it would have been useful to understand that planning was recursive, involving processes of replanning with new information, rather than creating one linear plan for their work. The researchers also suggested that increasing the range of strategies available for students may allow them to form new ideas about writing from sources and reinforce working in new and more productive ways. These strategies could include having students first discuss potential sources for their topics in order to see the task more broadly. It appears that students' writing and thinking were affected by their perceptions and interpretations of the task as well as by the context in which it occurred.

What Children Produce as They Write From Sources

In the research of Spivey and King (1989) report writing was the focus, and various analyses examined the composing outcomes of sixth, eighth, and tenth graders as they wrote from sources. The study investigated student reports written on the topic "rodeos," using encyclopedia entries intended for junior-high readers.

The findings highlighted the differences in children's ability to select appropriate content from sources. For example, eighth graders were more adept at selecting and chunking important information from references than sixth graders, and the tenth graders produced reports in which the ideas were more connected. The study further showed strong relations between reading ability across grade levels and writing on this task. Accomplished readers, regardless of grade level, wrote reports that were heavier in source content and more coherent. Their writings were integrated and showed well-developed structures. Less accomplished readers produced reports that contained less content and included information added by students but not drawn from references.

These findings suggest that accomplished readers make more skilled use of sources as they write reports and can frame new texts rather effectively. Linkages between writing and reading appear to manifest themselves in an ability, or lack thereof, to organize content across sources. The Spivey and King investigation also suggests some specific areas where less accomplished writers in middle school need support and strategy instruction in writing. These include ways to select important information from sources and synthesize information across reading materials.

The Connection Between Teacher Actions and Children's Writing and Thinking

When projects are the central focus of writing activity in content areas, the actions of the teacher can play a significant role in children's use of writing. Harper (1997) studied a literature-based third-grade classroom and looked at children's writing strategies and patterns of behavior in content-area projects in light of the models and instruction provided by the teacher. Each of the four case study children in this investigation demonstrated that they primarily "imitate text and format from models provided by the teacher, literature sources, and other students" (p. 178). Their composing often imitated what the teacher had written as a model, with similar format and types of sentences. Children's composing actions, for the most part, were *drafting*, or writing actual words onto the paper without hesitation, and *planning self-talk*. Their spurts of uninterrupted writing often were preceded by self-talk in which they announced what would be written or asked themselves questions. An example of composing close to the teacher's model is shown in the following excerpt.

In this lesson the teacher had produced on chart paper a large sample piece of writing about the U.S. Constitutional Convention. She talked to the class about their writing. Working independently, Kendra was writing about reasons for the colonists joining together. Her actions midway though a writing episode are coded at the left and her talk and writing are shown on the right.

Planning self-talk: K: I'm gonna put that was a good thing to do when they united.

Drafting: Writes *That was a good idea.*

Planning self-talk: K: Should I put what unite means? No...where does it? I don't want to put.... Oh, they met (looking at the chart).

Drafting, imitating text: Writes *They met in philadelphia, Pa.*

Planning self-talk: K: I've only got one page of Chapter One, but I'll bet I'll get more from this....Was it hard for George Washington? Yeh, it would have been to settle them down. Is George W. okay? I'll put Washington.

Drafting, imitating: Writes *George Washington lead the*

Planning self-talk: K: Unite. Would that make sense? No he led the...he led it? It?

Revision: Erases *the* and writes *it.* (p. 184)

In this brief excerpt Kendra uses self-talk to announce writing intentions and draws from the teacher's sample chart. Her writing-thinking actions show that she monitors for meaning using the supports provided.

In this study with third graders, imitation of text and models from the teacher predominated. The imitation rarely involved the writer synthesizing the given information into new and original pieces of work. It did, however, involve extended thinking about the concepts that were the project's focus. Harper concluded that the teacher's modeling of writing products was limiting for these learners. The children needed to consider various ways to produce their projects rather than reproducing a singular model.

Writing to Learn in Mathematics

Recent thinking in the area of mathematics for elementary- and middle-school children encourages the use of writing to support learning. Activities include keeping journals in mathematics to document processes for solving story problems, to consider mathematics concepts, and to reflect on personal progress in learning; and doing "process writing" of story problems so that children learn how such problems are constructed, written, and solved. Our understandings about writing and mathematics draw from work by Countryman (1992) and others and includes discussion of sharing sessions for student-written story problems and students' journal entries about learning. These studies highlight an interest in documenting ways that learners make connections between writing and the learning of mathematics concepts (Gordon & MacInnis, 1993).

A representative study in this area by Winograd (1993) looked at the writing processes of fifth graders as they produced original story problems and presented them in sharing sessions for their classmates to solve. Data collection for the study included students' think-aloud accounts as they wrote their story problems. Students were asked to say aloud everything that came to mind while writing. Data were gathered over 5 months as students participated in 3 to 4 periods weekly of story-problem writing.

The results documented three prevalent composing strategies for fifth-grade students. The first was *question directed*. Students seemed to say as they wrote story problems, "what will I write about" and "what is the question in this problem?" The process was recursive— moving back and forth from the emerging written text about the student's topic to the development of a culminating question and then back to include the necessary information needed to answer that question. For example:

Bruce:	Maybe I'll start with, um, I'm packing my stuff...even better than hiking, maybe I should...oh, I know...
Researcher:	What?
Bruce:	I'm gonna do about myself, how much stuff I need for hiking and how much money it's gonna cost. (p. 379)

These students, who were themselves effective problem solvers when working on the story problems of others, tended to monitor their problems in terms of whether they made sense and whether they provided information for solving the problem.

A second student strategy was *free association*. Less proficient writers focused on the topic itself, exploring what they could say and dealing with the culminating question after the text was nearly complete. These children mostly chose topics that were impersonal and not about lived-through experiences that could suggest problems or questions for the author. The free-association strategy allowed writers to explore and extend their topics, but did not seem associated with problem posing.

The third strategy was *intentionally increasing problem difficulty*. Students made a concerted effort to make the story problems difficult for their fellow students, adding among other things large numbers, extraneous information, and subprocedures to problems. Their think-alouds revealed trying to make the problems difficult but not impossible and reflected the high social status of constructing difficult problems within the classroom group.

The study closes with recommendations for mathematics teachers that map closely on practices for writing instruction. Among these are the following:

1. Children need models of the problems they are expected to write.
2. They need demonstrations about how to identify topics from their everyday lives.
3. Students need to have control over the content of their writing.
4. Story-problem writing needs to occur regularly and students need feedback from their audience.
5. Students need both conceptual and strategic knowledge to understand and solve mathematics problems.

Results of this study show similarities with research on writing instruction and children's composing. Of particular interest are the relations between planning that children do when writing mathematics problems and research about children's planning in writing generally.

Reading-Writing Connections

How Writing Influences Reading

The relations between writing and reading processes have been investigated from various perspectives. Those who have asked whether *writing influences reading* have looked at children's use of particular writing concepts as they engage in reading. For example, young children, through their invented or temporary spellings in writing, develop insights about letter-sound relations as they write their intended texts and grapple with various print concepts. They further explore these same concepts in books as they "read like a writer" (Smith, 1983), noticing conventional spellings and other features of print. Hansen (1987) describes this connection: "Writing is the foundation of reading...when our students write, they learn how reading is put together because they do it. They learn the essence of print" (pp. 178–179). Avery's (1993) book about first graders describes these writing-reading influences. She presents an unfolding documentary of action research, in which she carefully describes, from the first day of first grade, how her young students' reading and writing develops in concert and how "children naturally incorporate context, visual, and phonetic clues to decipher their own writing, then transfer these strategies to the reading of books by professional authors" (p. 381). More classroom research needs to be done across age and ability levels to explore the effect of writing and writing instruction on reading.

How Reading Influences Writing

Those who investigate how *reading influences writing* show that children's reading experiences are evident in the written texts they produce. Writers who participate in literature-based reading programs, for example, tend to produce writing with the structures and language features of their reading. Their written stories include dedication pages, illustrations, dots to indicate continuing events, and formulaic endings. Literature gives writers support for topics, word choices, spellings, story beginnings and endings, and illustrations.

When Eckhoff (1983) analyzed reading texts and writing samples in two second-grade classes, she discovered that literature seemed to have a direct influence on students' writing. The two classes used different basal series texts, one which matched more closely "the style and complexity of literary prose" (Basal A) and the other which used the "simplified style found in many basal reading texts" (Basal B) (p. 608). Eckhoff examined the writing style, format used in the writing, and linguistic structures of the students' writings. She discovered that although there was much variation among children's writing in both classes, there were also strong differences among the groups, which showed that the children's writings reflected features of the basal

81

series they were reading. For example, students reading the more complex text (Basal A) tended to use more elaborate and complex sentence structures including complex verb forms, subordinate clauses, and participial phrases, compared with the Basal B group who tended to use simpler sentence structures.

Regarding format and style, the basal readers again appeared to serve as models for writing. The Basal B group tended to write text in the form of one-line sentences that mirrored the way the basal text was written. The Basal B group also began sentences with *and* and ended them with *too* significantly more often than the Basal A group, reflecting a style frequently found in the basal series.

Eckhoff assumed that children in both classes had equal access to and knowledge of other works of literature. To test this assumption, she administered an inventory of children's books and, in fact, found that children in both classes had equal knowledge of children's literature. Eckhoff concluded that the children's writings were influenced by their classroom reading texts and commented, therefore, that children in elementary language arts classrooms would seem to benefit "from texts that help children learn to decode, and, at the same time, provide models representative of literary prose" (p. 616).

Writing and Literature

Children's literary responses have been the focus of extended theoretical writing by Rosenblatt (1989) who documents reader-text transactions and the ways that reader stance (guided by a reader's purpose for reading) affects literary events and responses. Further theoretical work by Sipe (1996) on primary-grade children's oral responses to picture books presents a typology of children's literary understandings. He describes three dimensions through which children's understandings can be seen:

1. Stance: How children situate themselves in relation to texts,
2. Action: What children do with texts, and
3. Function: How texts function.

He then describes five facets of children's literary understanding across these dimensions:

1. Within texts, children analyze, using texts as objects.

2. Across texts, children link or relate, using texts as context.

3. From or to texts, children personalize, using texts as stimuli.

4. Through texts, children merge with texts, using texts as their identity.

5. On texts, children perform or "signify," using texts as platforms. (p. 253)

This typology suggests that children analyze stories and consider the characteristics of books—their endpages, illustrations, story events, and characters. Children talk about plots and story endings, link stories to other literary works, and describe connections across authors or genres. As they interact with stories, children personalize them by making life-to-story or story-to-life connections. In this domain the story functions as a platform for children's creativity and becomes a significant playground for the imagination. Although this typology is grounded in research involving first and second graders' oral discussions of picture books in a literature-based program, it is interesting to consider whether these literary understandings can be seen in children's self-sponsored writing and whether their written responses to literature demonstrate the dimensions of literary understandings.

The body of research about writing and literature includes few recent studies exploring children's own writing and their literary understandings. Research is needed to explore possible connections between the literary knowledge evident in children's written productions and the literary insights children demonstrate when they are being read to or are reading on their own. However, there are studies investigating literary response journals that look at how children respond in writing to their reading experiences. Bagge-Rynerson (1994) reports that, although her first- and second-grade students participated in lively discussions about literature, they viewed journals as ways that adults monitored whether they had completed their reading. Literary journals in this classroom were lifeless and brief; they seemed to go stale and did not serve as vehicles for reflection or personal response.

The adjustments made to this literature writing assignment were to ask for fewer entries (one for every three books read), have the teacher model the kinds of entries that could be written, and provide some structure for children needing support. The following list of questions was available to help children who needed prompts:

Does this story remind you of anything that has ever happened to you?

If you were in the story would you do the same thing that the main character did?

Is there a character that you would like to have as a friend?

Does this book remind you of anything else that you have read?

What do you think the author is trying to tell you?

If you had a chance to talk to the author or illustrator, what would you say or ask?

How did the words or pictures in the book make you feel? (p. 93)

The teacher also adjusted her own manner of responding to written entries. Instead of questioning the young readers, she wrote responses that validated their responses and also wrote about her own reactions to the story. The procedures also shifted from using journals for dialogue to talking with individual children about their journals during reading conferences.

Hancock (1993) investigated sixth graders' literary responses in journals, looking at what children wrote in journals about four award-winning realistic fiction books, the nature of their responses, and how their literary understandings unfolded over time. The instructions for the response journals were for children "to record everything that is rambling through your mind as you read the book" (p. 340). Other data included observations and interviews with students.

Results from analyzing journal entries showed that students grappled with both the business of making sense of the story as it unfolded and their own urge to become involved personally. Students also wrote journal entries that reflected an evaluative stance and wrote about the literary works and their own perspective on reading and writing. These responses were categorized as follows:

Immersion: understanding, predicting, questioning, and character introspection.

Self-Involvement: identifying with characters, assessing characters, and being involved in the story.

Detachment: literary evaluation, reader-writer digressions.

Journal responses in this study varied widely across learners. One student functioned as a literary critic writing evaluations of each author's work; another was an intense reader who became deeply involved in each story and wrote lengthy responses to specific characters. The researcher concluded that readers' responses were diverse and each reader had a unique way of responding to literature. These individual approaches to meaning making changed markedly from one book to another for some children, while others had consistent ways of responding across separate book experiences.

This research shows students constructing their written literary understandings in many of the same ways described in research on children's discussions (Sipe, 1996). Students analyzed across texts and used texts as stimuli for their own personalized roles. Children's writing showed them entering the world of the story.

These studies connecting writing and literature affirm the notion that writing can serve as a reflective tool and as a way of personally responding to literary works. It is important to consider how the intertwining of writing and literature shapes children's writing. The studies described here have reported only journal writing—writing about literature. Writing and literature connections need to be studied in which children are both the readers of specific literature and producers of original works.

Transactions Between Writing and Reading

The body of research showing *writing and reading as transacting processes* (each process concurrently changing the other and being changed in the process) looks at the generative nature of both processes. When writers reread their own work with their audience in mind, they reshape ideas in their intended text and discover new ones. Students working in genre studies (for example, reading the poetry of other authors and writing their own poems) extend their range of ideas and writing options as they read and write. The transactive relation between writing and reading leads to critical insights across texts as students generate and express new meanings.

In addition to these trends, the body of writing-reading research includes some central concepts that are critical for understanding these relations. These concepts are listed following along with citations of exemplary studies.

- Reading and writing are each enhanced when they are taught and learned together and when learners draw upon information from both processes (Shanahan & Lomax, 1986).

- Proficient readers and writers actively control their actions and shift strategies as they construct and monitor meaning (Birnbaum, 1982).

- Reading and writing are similar in many aspects but differ in patterns of cognitive behaviors across processes and in learner approaches during meaning making (Langer, 1986b).

- Reading and writing as processes both involve the construction of text worlds from prior knowledge, personal meanings, and relations discovered through reading writing engagements (Kucer, 1985).

- To enhance thinking and learning from multiple perspectives the combination of reading and writing is more effective than either process alone (Tierney, Soter, O'Flahavan, & McGinley, 1989).

- The strategies used by students writing from their reading across multiple sources varies widely from one learner to another (McGinley, 1992).

Looking across this body of research, it is particularly interesting to consider what writing-reading relations mean for classroom teachers in literature-based programs. In these classrooms, students move back and forth seamlessly between writing and reading as they engage in responding to literature and creating literary works of their own.

Classroom Implications and Ideas for Instruction

Earlier in this chapter, we made the statement that a natural link exists between writing and thinking. Given the existing research on writing-thinking relations, there is a strong argument for using writing across the curriculum to support learning. Learning logs or journals, for example, provide one way to use writing for learning. It appears, however, that it is important for the writing to be purposeful and extend beyond simply copying or summarizing. Students can be asked to reflect on a discussion or a reading and to write about those reflections. They can be asked to elaborate on ideas and information presented, and perhaps to evaluate the information against specific criteria. In other words, if the writing-thinking connection is to be productive for children, it must involve an active generation of ideas and concepts. The writing must involve young learners in the construction of meaning—their own meaning.

One area in which writing seems particularly to have potential for promoting learning is mathematics. When students write about their problem solving, they are making their thought processes explicit—for themselves as well as their teacher. The writing provides a system of feedback to inform young learners about their understandings of mathematical processes. When children write their own word problems, they focus their attention on the application of numbers and mathematical concepts to events and situations. The thinking and writing focus the learner's attention on how those concepts can be used to answer questions and draw conclusions.

There is also a natural link between writing and the reading of literature. Through writing, young children learn about language, how it appears in print, and how the sounds of language map onto the graphic symbols. Through reading, children learn about print conventions and language structures and can transfer that learning to their writing. Literature serves as a model for language use, sentence construction, style, and format and teachers have long recognized the value of quality literature as a critical element in children's literacy development. In addition, writing provides a venue for young readers' reflections about their reading, reflections that help them clarify and deepen their understandings of what they have read.

At the heart of our discussion on writing-reading relations is the young learner, whose intentions and purposes seem to be paramount when they are using writing to construct meaning. This seems to be especially true when they are reading and writing from a variety of sources. The most common task of this kind is the research report or report of information. It appears that how young learners perceive or interpret the task strongly affects how they approach the research and writing. If the objective is for children to transform information, rather than merely transcribe it, then young learners must understand the purpose of their work.

Here, we refer not to the teacher's purpose, but to the learner's purpose. Why are the children doing the research? Do they have an inquiry focus that is important to them? Do they feel ownership for the task? What are their perceptions regarding *why* they are doing a task, the effectiveness of *how* they are doing it, and *strategies* they might use to more effectively solve a particular problem or answer a question?

Looking Ahead

In terms of writing-reading relations, we need studies across the range of ages—from first through eighth grade. Critical questions include the following: What are the developmental aspects of the relations between reading and writing and how do these relations between reading and writing change as students gain proficiency? What instructional conditions in reading promote the development of writing? And what conditions in writing instruction promote development in reading?

Many of these same questions can be asked within the context of writing and thinking. Although Langer and Applebee's study focused on older students, how might their findings about the relations between writing and learning processes be similar or different for younger students? What are the writing-learning strategies that proficient students use in comparison with struggling students engaging in writing to learn?

Although writing and doing mathematics tend to be viewed as skills at opposite ends of a spectrum, educators have begun exploring the myriad connections between the two. Certainly, there is more work to be done in this area, not just connecting what we know about writing processes and the writing of story problems, but also taking a comprehensive look at the possible contributions that writing about mathematics can make to children's learning. Are there other writing activities that might enhance mathematics learning? How might writing about mathematics contribute to a child's language, writing, and reading development?

Another area for future research centers on writing from sources, the sine qua non of school writing—a way in which students demonstrate both knowledge and writing ability. Yet, many questions remain about what constitutes successful writing practices for young writers grappling with multiple sources and adjusting their concepts of planning, organizing, and composing: What strategies need to be taught to support these writing efforts? What social dimensions need to be explored as children write collaboratively in extended projects? These questions take on increasing importance with the advent of technology and the Internet. As children increasingly explore the World Wide Web for information and ideas, it will be critical to support them in the task of constructing knowledge from this immense and complex resource. (See the next chapter for a discussion of writing and technology.)

In addition to writing from sources, writing about literature has been a mainstay of traditional writing tasks. Literary response journals document individual responses and ideas, allowing for individual lived-through experiences in reading a literary work to be expressed in writing. Yet many questions remain about how children write about literature and how writing can become a form of reading engagement. The issues of classroom conditions and strategies are important in this area, also.

We propose that research consider not only writing *about* literature, but also writing *through* literature. It is important to know how literary understandings develop across both reading and writing experiences as children work in reading and writing workshops or engage in genre studies. What are the influences of literary experiences and understandings on children's writing? How do these literary understandings in writing and reading develop across the grades?

Finally, researchers need to explore writing and learning as children work in comprehensive themed units that integrate several subject areas on a broad scale. These themed experiences, which might be based on a problem, a question, or a topic, place children in contexts in which subject areas come together and writing serves as a vehicle for learning in collaborative contexts. What do children learn about writing when classroom instruction integrates science, math, social studies, and literature? What kinds of writing and thinking do children experience within these integrated studies?

Writing appears to have the potential for playing a powerful role in the classroom. There are implications in the teaching of writing that extend beyond learning the construction of linguistic structures, although that construction is certainly critical to writing. The better we understand the role of writing and the nature of its impact, the more effective we can become at supporting children's development in literacy and learning.

CHAPTER 6

Technology and Writing

For many children in the United States, computer access in school is sporadic and writing is carried out primarily with paper and pencil. In spite of this fact, technology is playing an increasingly important role in instruction and learning. This chapter discusses the growing role of technology in learning environments, what we know about elementary- and middle-school writers and computer usage, and what questions remain yet to be answered. For example, we take a look at how word processing affects children's composing processes and how the technology itself can alter those processes.

Although it may sound overly dramatic to say this, computers and technology are changing the world in ways unprecedented in history. Because of the nature of today's technological advances, the content of this chapter provides only a glimpse into what is the largely unexplored territory of rapidly changing technology and its potential effects on reading and writing education.

It is impossible to predict exactly where technology will lead us as we approach the 21st century. We can speculate, but exact predictions are no more possible here than they were in the early 20th century when the first cars clambered over uneven roads, eliciting stares from people sitting astride their horse-drawn carriages.

Who could have predicted even a decade ago the advent of the World Wide Web (WWW)? The Internet, of which the WWW is only a portion, has only a 30-year history. It began in the 1960s when individuals at the Rand Corporation, under the leadership of Paul Baran, created an innovative communications network designed to ensure that military communications would not be interrupted even in the midst of battle. Baran's recommendations, although not acted on by the Pentagon, influenced subsequent work that connected four universities in the United States with one another, a network that eventually grew into the information superhighway called the Internet, a huge network of networks, which covers the entire globe. (See the Web site at http://www.pbs.org/internet/ to read more about the history of the Internet.)

Technology and New Learning Environments

Where will technology take those of us who are involved in education tomorrow? How will it change us, our interactions with one another, our vocabularies, and our ways of thinking? There is talk of virtual universities, where no ground is broken for new buildings and where no classrooms or professors' offices exist. In fact, there is a "virtual" high school, Virtual High in Vancouver, British Columbia, a private school with approximately 25 students enrolled at any one time. The curriculum is completely learner centered: Students set their own agendas for learning and decide what curriculum they want to study, and by connecting to the school's computer network, students can do all of their work online at home.

Entire learning environments are being designed around technology. One of the most interesting and well-researched technologically based learning environments is the Computer Supported Intentional Learning Environment (CSILE), begun in 1986 in Toronto by researchers in cognition and computer science. Scardamalia and Bereiter (1996), key researchers in the project, describe this environment as "a network of networks—people from schools, universities, cultural institutions, service organizations, businesses—simultaneously building knowledge within their primary groups while advancing the knowledge of others" (p. 6). The participants refer to this evolving model as a "knowledge society," an interactive knowledge-building and knowledge-sharing community that directly involves children in K–12 schools, preservice and inservice teachers, scientists, entrepreneurs, medical school students, and many others. Concerns in this environment are not unlike concerns in any learning situation. Does it offer the kind of involvement in which all participants benefit and in which all are "constructing, using, and improving knowledge" (p. 9), fifth graders as well as highly expert research scientists? Are the processes scaleable, that is, can they be made available to more than a few well-equipped classrooms? Are the processes sustainable, not requiring unreasonable effort and volunteer time from a select few individuals who are likely to become overworked? These are questions CSILE researchers and participants are asking and attempting to answer.

One other issue is central to electronic learning environments: Exactly what role does technology play? Bill Gates, founder of Microsoft, answers this question with some authority in his autobiography *The Road Ahead* (1995). He says that the "information highway" will never replace expert and committed teachers, capable administrators, involved parents, and hardworking students. In the CSILE project, this question has been answered similarly. Technology's role is to facilitate the construction of knowledge, and it is human effort that is at the center of the knowledge society model. For example, the researchers cite preservice teachers as being a critical element as they are involved in teaching, in guiding, and in continuing their own learning. To date, research from CSILE indicates that students who are a part of this knowledge society excel in a variety of ways, from showing sophisticated insights about learning to performing better on standardized reading and language tests.

The only certain and predictable aspect of technology seems to be change itself. Some might point to the invention of bookmaking technologies in the mid–15th century as a time of rapid and significant change. There is no doubt that this technology changed the lives of individuals and affected the development of societies and cultures. However, although the uses of bookmaking technology were dramatically expanded from the first printings of the Bible and processes associated with the technology became much more sophisticated, the end result—the printing of books—remained relatively stable for hundreds of years. The same cannot be said for today's electronic technologies. The future is open, and innovations are being revealed at a startlingly fast pace.

The Role of Technology in Writing

There is a danger in writing this chapter. Two decades ago, it probably would not have been included in a book of this type. Only one decade ago, its content would have been quite different. Now, technology is changing so rapidly that there is danger that in some respects it may be obsolete before it is printed. Still, we believe it is important to look at the current status of what we know regarding the complex relation between writing and technology.

We emphasize the word *complex*. There was a time when the computer was seen by educators as simply a tool through which writing could occur. The computer would merely facilitate writing through word-processing software; once writers had a modicum of keyboard expertise they could simply substitute the computer for a pen or pencil, thereby making various revision work and editing less of a chore. Educators and researchers did not look at the writing, which, it was supposed, was carried out in much the same manner regardless of the writing implement. Instead, their focus was on how the computer, as a tool, brought a degree of ease into the writing process, an ease that students typically did not experience as they wrote, revised, and edited their work with pen or pencil and paper.

In the 1980s however, researchers began to examine the complexity inherent in the relation between writing and technology. Ong (1982) suggested that using technologies actually transforms our consciousness, that the technology itself may transform our ways of thinking and writing, and our ways of knowing and making meaning. Ong reminds us of Plato's argument that writing itself is an inhuman, alienating technology that destroys memory, violating the sanctity of what is in the mind. A similar argument has been made that computer technology is inhuman, inhumane, and somehow counterproductive to thinking and learning.

Agreeing with Ong, McDaniel commented in her 1987 bibliography on the growing number of computer-assisted composition (CAC) software that a common element exists among the technologies of writing, printing, and computing. The element found in these technologies is that they all have significant effects on thinking and communication:

> The truly substantial influences of printing, like those of writing, were long in developing but ultimately affected human thought, learning, and expression—the text maker and the making, not simply the text itself. Now, technology's effect on literacy concerns us again as we inspect the densest technology yet to come between idea and expression, imagination and form, thinker and composer. (p. 139)

Research on Technology in the Classroom

LeBlanc presents a thorough picture of the world of CAC software in his 1993 book written specifically for teachers of writing. He makes the point that computer technology is simply unavoidable, that it has "invaded the classroom, workplace, and home with dizzying speed" (p. 3). He cites the fact that over 95% of public schools currently have computers and that the student-to-computer ratio grew from 92 to 1 in 1983, to 26 to 1 in 1993. Considering the growing presence of technology, LeBlanc argues convincingly that teachers must have a voice in designing the software that writers will use in computer-supported environments.

> If we wish to take a proactive role in the shaping of electronic literacy, software design should be as mainstream an activity of composition professionals as teaching a writing class, conducting a research study, or writing an article. (p. 10)

LeBlanc also describes who is developing CAC software, and how; trends that are emerging in software development; and implications of the use of writing software on the field of composition. That these software systems have the potential to directly shape processes of writing is seen in one software program LeBlanc presents as an example, Anne and Mike DiPardo's HyperCard-based CAC system. This system allows users to make complex links among ideas, where students "write essays with built-in buttons which open up windows that would include students' asides, further explanations, and other information they wish to link out from the text" (LeBlanc, 1993, p. 74). In addition, the links could contain screens and activities that would help guide writers through the composing processes. These links might do such things as pose questions to encourage writers' rereading of and reflection on ideas presented, spark brainstorming, and offer sample essays that highlight, for example, introductions or endings. Clearly, this software system affects how writers think about their writing by encouraging certain processes and activities. The writing is definitely shaped by the technology.

Haas's Research: Comparing Pen and Paper With Computers

In an attempt to understand how technology affects writing, Christina Haas has done extensive work on differences between writing with computers and with pen and paper. In several studies (1989a, 1989b), she discovered that experienced writers actually planned less when writing short expository pieces (two to five pages) with the computer, as opposed to when using pen and paper. In the studies, it appeared that the computer affected the way writers approached the writing task, influencing their composing processes.

Relevant to Haas's work is research that suggests that, regardless of whether writers are using pen and paper or a computer, there are differences in novice and experienced writers' predrafting notetaking. Young, less experienced writers' prewriting notes often became the compositions themselves, without significant editing or reorganizing. In contrast, among older, more experienced writers, notes offered ideas that were then expanded on and reorganized to provide a basis for the composing; the composition was expanded to be much more than the predrafting notes themselves (Burtis, Scardamalia, Bereiter, & Tetroe, 1983). These findings were similar to those of Bereiter and Scardamalia (1987), who found that elementary-school writers tended to be much less effective at planning their compositions than were more experienced writers.

What are the effects on writing when computer technology enters the scene? In one particular study, Haas (1990) found that there were no differences, whether using a computer or pen and paper, in the number of notes that writers made. There were, however, significant differences in the kinds of notes they made. With pen and paper, writers tended to make a variety of different notes. Some, for example, had to do with the structure of the essay. These notes contained arrows and other graphics that helped writers think about the organization of the essay. They tended to contain brief phrases organized into categories that helped writers conceptualize chunks of content. With the computer, notes tended to be more textlike and to be focused almost exclusively on content rather than on the content and its organization. Haas concluded that the medium did, indeed, influence these experienced writers' processes.

She further concluded that there is much research yet to be done on the effect of computers on writers' processes. She acknowledged that her study examined two extremes: writers using only pen and paper or using only computers for notetaking. She speculated that the effect might be different if writers used both. She also stated that the research highlighted a need for writing software that would support critical functions of planning and monitoring writing, as well as editing. This may be especially crucial for young, developing writers who tend, by virtue of their novice status, to bring less planning into their composing processes than do more experienced writers.

Reviews of Research on Computers and Writing

Several researchers have conducted extensive reviews in which they examined what research studies tell us about the effects of computer technology on writing. In one comprehensive review of research that focused on word processing and elementary writers, Cochran-Smith (1991) concluded that the effect of word processing is not straightforward, that it depends on many factors, such as writers' keyboarding skills and previous experience with computers, teachers' instructional goals and perspectives regarding technology, and the organization of the classroom. In her review of the literature, Cochran-Smith reported that keyboarding and computer expertise do not appear, by themselves, to be significant factors influencing students' writing through word processing. However, she did report that time is needed for some students to become comfortable with use of the computer and that time constraints and students' levels of comfort may affect how they use the computer for writing. She emphasized that teachers represent a key variable in terms of what instructional strategies for thinking and writing they implement along with word processing. Similarly, Russell (1991), in a meta-analysis of 21 studies that researched the effects of word processing on student writing, found the relation between technology and writing to be complex and cautioned that the social interactions in computer labs may be as responsible for increased quality in writing as the word-processing technology itself.

Cochran-Smith, Paris, and Kahn (1991) also emphasized the importance of considering context and multiple variables related to students, teachers, classrooms, and communities when studying effects of computer technology on student writing. However, they ventured that, regardless of context, several conclusions regarding writing and computers could be drawn. These conclusions are that students who write with word-processing software tend to make more revisions, write longer compositions, and produce text that is freer of the surface errors associated with conventions and mechanics, compared with students who write with pen and pencil. Cochran-Smith et al. (1991) also stated that students tend to have more positive attitudes toward writing when they use technology, although other research has not always supported this conclusion.

Another review of research was conducted by Bangert-Drowns (1993), who analyzed 32 studies, each of which specifically compared two groups of students receiving identical instruction in writing. These studies were conducted with various sample groups, including elementary school, middle and high school, and college students. In each study, one group used word processing for writing, while the other group used pen and paper. His review was motivated by an understanding that "the computer as a tool, as a spread sheet, database, network link graphics generator, calculator, and word processor is transforming the way the 'information age' society lives and works" (p. 70). Educators must therefore take a close look at the educational benefits of these tools. In his meta-analysis, Bangert-Drowns examined the effects of technology use on four measures: writing quality, amount of writing (number of words), frequency of revision, and effective use of conventions.

Regarding quality, Bangert-Drowns's analysis showed that a majority of the studies reported increased writing quality with word processing, although many of these increases were small. Students' quality of writing before instruction could, to a degree, predict the quality of their writing after instruction; nevertheless, the postinstruction writing-quality indicators were significantly higher for the word-processing groups. Also, the less skilled writers tended to benefit more from word processing than did the medium and higher skilled students. Bangert-Drowns speculates about why this might be: He suggests that perhaps less skilled writers, who have been disengaged from writing tasks, might find increased motivation in using word processing to write. He further speculates that this increased motivation may lead to more positive attitudes toward writing in the groups of students using word processing.

In fact, this is not what he found in his analysis. On the contrary, he found that more positive attitudes toward writing do not seem to be a requirement for students' increased engagement and writing quality. Perhaps, he suggests, students are more willing to work with computers for writing than they are to work with pen and paper because the computer engages them more effectively, meaning they are willing to work harder. This conclusion may be supported by the fact that word-processing students generally wrote longer compositions than those writing with pen and paper. In addition, there was a strong correlation between the longer writings and those that were judged to be of higher quality.

Regarding students' use of writing conventions, their ability to exercise a high degree of mechanical control in their writing, Bangert-Drowns's meta-analysis found that 7 of 12 studies that looked at conventions reported positive outcomes. However, the size of the effect was so low that it did not differ significantly from zero effect. In addition, mixed results were seen in correlations between writing quality and effective use of conventions. In all, the correlation was virtually zero.

One other finding from this meta-analysis is that results regarding students' revisions did not appear to shed any light on the impact of word processing versus writing with pen and paper. Most of the studies counted the number of revisions, which were often difficult to track when students made changes using the computer, as they did not all show up as differences from first to final copies. Bangert-Drowns suggested that perhaps instead of counting frequency of changes from first to final draft, a better way to track revisions with word processing would be to count keystrokes or conduct direct observations of the writing-revising processes.

In this analysis, the study with the largest reported effect in terms of revision was one in which all students wrote their final copies with pen and paper. Therefore, their revisions were more visible. Also, this meta-analysis found that studies in which students had worked previously with software that helped them analyze text reported more revisions, whether students were using the computer or pen and paper.

Bangert-Drowns offers an explanation for these results, particularly those regarding conventions and revisions. None of the studies he analyzed made special instructional adjustments for the use of word processing, and the act of using word processing does not, in itself, appear to result in marked improvement in writing. As in any learning environment, the context, the identification of explicit learning goals, the design of instruction, opportunities for practice, and other variables affect outcomes.

Elementary-School Writers and Technology

We turn our attention now to a more focused discussion of young children and the use of technology in writing. Dickinson's (1986) research in a first- and second-grade classroom provides insights about ways in which technology can affect writing and classroom social organization. When computers were integrated into this classroom, the teacher envisioned using them for writing, and particularly for projects in the social studies curriculum. What the teacher and researcher discovered was that children began increasingly to ask to work together at the computer. The computer screen may have allowed students' writings, and thus their ideas, to be more accessible to one another. As students became increasingly collaborative when they wrote on the computer, their talk began to include discussions of planning what to write, self-monitoring comments (for example, discussions of spelling), and responses to one another's ideas and writing content. This was in marked contrast to the singular nature of these first and second graders' writing experiences when they used pencil and paper at their desks.

These findings are similar to those of Bruce, Michaels, and Watson-Gegeo (1985), who discovered that sixth graders became more collaborative in their writing when they worked on computers. The researchers speculated that the public nature of the computer screen encouraged students to comment on one another's writing as they walked around the classroom, stood in line, and waited for the teacher to answer questions.

Jones and Pellegrini (1996) examined the effect of word processing on the writing of first graders. They found that word processing, when compared with paper and pencil writing, facilitated these students' writing of narratives. They speculated that the technology took the emphasis away from the mechanical aspects of writing, allowing children to focus on words and ideas. The students' narratives written with word-processing software were more cohesive, the cohesiveness accomplished through repetition and word choice. This is not surprising when considered in relation to another finding from this study. The researchers found that children used more metacognitive language when they used the computer than when they used paper and pencil; they focused and reflected more on their ideas and language use.

Another study involving a very young, developing writer is a case study of a 5-year-old writing with word-processing software (Cochran-Smith, Kahn, & Paris, 1990). The researchers found writing with pencil and paper versus writing with word processing to be a qualitatively different experience for this child. It appeared that the computer provided a tool that supported the child's developing writing skills. Word processing seemed to deemphasize her mechanical concerns of such things as handwriting, letter formation, and alignment of words. Instead, the technology seemed to support the notion that writing was about "verbal composition" (p. 240), that it was about words and ideas.

In addition, word processing seemed to provide an environment in which a writing coach or teacher's aide could work productively with the child. The coach was able to intervene more *during* the writing, rather than after. The child shifted her attention to letter-sound correspondence, content, and organization, and away from the purely physical and mechanical aspects of writing. Word processing seemed to create opportunities and a social context in which this young writer could approach the writing differently than when using pencil and paper. The researchers caution, however, that with some 5- to 10-year-olds, word processing seemed to interfere with the writing. An explanation may be that these children may have been more uncomfortable with their developing writing skills than with the computer technology.

Adolescent Writers and Technology

Owston, Murphy, and Wideman (1992) conducted a study to determine the effects of word processing on eighth-grade students' writing quality and revision strategies. The study was motivated by the fact that most research has been conducted with older students (that is, high school and college) and little research had been done with middle-school students' writing and technology. Although there is some research with intermediate-grade and middle-school students that shows an increase in quality of writing with the use of word processing, that body of work is not extensive. One study conducted in 1991 with narrative writing (Owston, Murphy, & Wideman) found that stories were judged to be significantly better when written with word processing than with pen and paper. Students in the 1992 study were all experienced computer users, and the work focused on expository writing.

Results of this research showed that students using word process-ing wrote higher quality essays. In terms of length, word processing did not produce significantly longer papers than pen and paper did. However, there was more variability in length with word processing. In order to determine whether the differences in quality ratings might be explained by spelling differences, the researchers examined 100 papers at random, half of which were handwritten and half of which were written through word processing. They found no significant dif-ferences in spelling across the two groups.

ScreenRecorder software recorded data for 19 students in Owston et al.'s 1992 study. The objective was to track revisions made by stu-dents using word processing. They found that students revised throughout their writing, but that they did most revising during their initial drafting, perhaps when they felt that their texts were less final-ized and cast in stone. They also made more small, microstructural changes to text than large changes that involved major restructuring and reorganization.

The researchers hypothesized that one element that may have had a significant effect on student writing was students' expertise with computers, with word-processing software and all of the options it af-fords to writers regarding editing and text manipulation. The word-pro-cessing software they used was Microsoft Works, which allowed for fairly easy manipulation of functions through pulldown menus and mouse-controlled functions, as is typical of most word-processing soft-ware today. Haas (1989a) found with older students that word-pro-cessing software that used functions similar to that of Microsoft Works resulted in higher quality compositions than software that requires key-board commands for every function that might be found on tradition-al PCs. It makes sense that the choice of software would be even more critical for younger writers, for whom cognitively demanding software might interfere with writing processes.

Daiute (1986) also studied revision strategies of middle-school stu-dents when they used word processing. She found that students cor-rected more errors with word processing than with pen and paper. She also found that their revisions were substantially different with word processing. Students tended to make additions to a writing, usually by adding more at the end, when using word processing. Interestingly, the computer drafts were often shorter than paper and pen drafts. However, revisions of the drafts eventually resulted in longer writings with word processing. Although, as Owston et. al. (1992) found, word processing did not result in students making larger textual revisions in the form of restructuring or reorganization. Dauite found that writing software that used prompts to make cognitive processes explicit and open to reflection guided students to significantly improve their revision strategies, including more consideration of reorganization and elaboration. She did not find this to be true when students used word processing that did not include the prompts.

One reason that young writers do not tend to revise globally when word processing may have to do with the computer screen. The writer can read only what is on the screen and does not have the benefit of rereading text except within the limits allowed by the hardware. This may interfere with revisions that involve significant structural and content changes (Hawisher, 1986). Through interviews with computer users, Haas (1989c) found a large number of reports that the users did not have a "sense of the text" (p. 24). In other words, students were frustrated in their ability to engage in "the kind of self-critical reading that is crucial for successful writing and revising" (p. 24). This seems to be a problem particularly when writers are constructing text as they compose, rather than when they are writing something that is already fairly well formulated in their minds beforehand.

Writing of Special Needs Students and Technology

One other area to explore in terms of the interrelation between computers and writing is that of special needs students. Morocco (1987) reported the effect of word processing on the writing of learning disabled (LD) students using programs that included such metacognitive aids as procedural instructions and prompts to support reflections regarding structures and frameworks for writing. She concluded that such word-processing software helped these students work with text, particularly with entering and deleting ideas. In addition, it helped teachers by making more visible the procedures and processes that students were using, thus making it easier to provide support for their writing.

Morocco, Dalton, and Tivnan (1992) documented the positive effects of spelling and grammar checkers on the writing of fourth-grade LD students. Similar to previous research described in this chapter, research with LD children points to the conclusion that instruction is a crucial variable. Storeyard, Simmons, Stumpf, and Pavloglou (1993) reported on the success of word processing for eighth-grade students with learning disabilities. Their teacher integrated strategy lessons such as brainstorming and webbing into the writing program, with positive results on her students' writing. In addition, as with very young students, the computer encourages collaboration among young writers with special needs, as well as between teacher and student (Montague & Graves, 1993), thus providing opportunities for advising and feedback, prompting of reflection, and discussion of ideas.

With the knowledge that word processing appears to be a potentially valuable tool for students with learning disabilities, one large-scale study attempted to discern what difficulties these students might encounter when using the computer for writing. Lewis, Ashton, and Kieley (1996) were interested in barriers that word processing might present to LD students, particularly barriers associated with text entry. They wondered whether the computer keyboard was an impediment to writing when compared with handwriting for these students. Not surprisingly, when compared with a control group that continued writing by hand, the technology groups' fluency in writing (rate of text entry) dropped by about half. However, the researchers did find variations on the speed of text entry from the effects of different technologies used by groups of students. The technology groups consisted of (1) a group that used word processing only and the standard QWERTY keyboard; (2) a group that used word processing and also received instruction in keyboarding; (3) a group that used word processing and an alternate keyboard with keys arranged in alphabetical order; (4) a group that used a word-prediction program, Co:Writer, to enter text; and (5) a group that used Co:Writer with the speech synthesis feature activated. These treatments were implemented over the course of one academic year with LD students in Grades 4 through 12.

Results from this research favored the fourth group which used the word-prediction feature (although without the speech feature, which students and teachers felt slowed students significantly). Students in the word-prediction group had the highest posttest text entry speed (82% of the pretest); showed improved writing accuracy, especially in spelling; and showed improved writing quality. The next most effective technologies involved the group using the QWERTY keyboard and the word-processing group receiving instruction in keyboarding. These two groups increased their text entry speed from pre- to posttest by 74%, and both groups' writing accuracy increased, particularly with respect to spelling improvement. However, students' overall writing quality increased only in the QWERTY group.

The researchers recommended that several factors be considered when choosing a text-entry strategy for LD students:

1. Consider the ease with which a strategy can be used—for the teacher as well as for students.

2. Make sure that the computers' capabilities are sufficient for the software being used.

3. Consider students' attitudes toward the strategy. It could be counterproductive if students think the strategy is "babyish."

4. Realize that speed, by itself, is not the only objective. It is possible that speed of text entry can decrease while writing quality increases.

5. Some students might do well with more than one technology strategy for writing.

6. Monitor students' progress carefully and make adjustments as needed.

In summary, evidence is accumulating that writing with computer support tends to make writing easier for young children whose writing skills are in the initial phases of development, as well as intermediate-level and young adolescent students across ability levels. Evidence is also accumulating regarding the many variables that can affect the relation between technology and writing. These are the issues that require further exploration to create increasingly effective use of technology for young writers. In the next section we provide an annotated bibliography of selected Web sites that contain information about writing for teachers and students.

Web Sites to Browse

The Internet is accessible to anyone with access to the appropriate equipment, a little bit of know-how, and a sufficient interest to be a part of the network. Sites are posted on the Web for all to see by individuals who meet only these three criteria, and they are virtually unedited and uncensored. In addition, if the creator of the site decides to remove it from a particular spot on the Web identified by the URL (Uniform Resource Locator), it will disappear, often not leaving a forwarding address. With the caveat that the sites may have moved, we have included in this chapter some Web pages we think might be interesting to teachers and researchers of writing.

For teachers of writing: http://www-gse.berkeley.edu/Research/NWP/nwp.html

Visit the National Writing Project homepage, and from there visit sites of National Writing Projects (NWP) across the United States. From this homepage, teachers have access to publications offered by the NWP and to the new NWP online newsletter, *Voices*, where they can give input to topics they would like to see addressed in subsequent issues. One site on the homepage is called Teacher Researcher On-Line. This site provides resources and bibliographies as well as a place to read about work other teacher researchers are doing in writing.

For young writers and their teachers: http://www.inkspot.com

This Web site is a highly useful resource for young writers and their teachers. From this site, young writers can be a part of a forum to exchange ideas with one another and with experienced writers. This page is linked to a site for writers of children's books and to a collection of works by young writers in the Young Writers' Showcase. Students can read works by other young writers and can also submit their writings to be published on the Web. There is an advice column called "Dear Kathy," where young writers can ask questions about writing that are answered by a professional writer. "Dear Kathy" is the author of *Market Guide for Young Writers*. This site is informative and useful and offers something for teachers who are writers, as well as for children and adolescent writers.

For young adolescents and teenagers: http://www.writes.org/netscape/about_wp/guide.html

This Web site is called Writes of Passage, described as an outlet for teenagers "that inspires communication through reading and writing." This is an electronic literary journal, designed for adolescents from ages 12 to 19 as a place for teens to communicate with peers, to improve their writing, and to have their writing published. Adolescents can be a part of conversations with writers such as Robert Cormier and Mary Higgins Clark. There is also a Teachers' Guide designed to aid in the teaching of poetry and creative writing, with lesson plans, many of which are built around student writings.

For young writers: http://www.kidpub.org/kidpub/intro.html

KidPub is a delightful site where there are "more than 8000 stories written by kids from all over the planet." The author of this site originally intended to create a place to encourage his 9-year-old daughter to write and be a part of the Internet. It has become an exciting site where children can learn about HTML (Hypertext Mark-up Language) formatting and publish their own stories on the Web. Children and their teachers can visit schools that have participated in KidPub writing projects, and read some of the stories they have submitted. Children can participate in a chat area for KidPub authors and can also become Internet Keypals with other young writers.

Classroom Implications and Ideas for Instruction

When considering the role of technology in writing and writing instruction, we believe it is important to emphasize that technology is a tool to support learning—in this case thinking and writing. A computer cannot write for students; it can only be used *for* writing. Because computers are becoming an integral part of the world, we believe that students should have access to this technology. However, as in classrooms without technology, the classroom environment, the teacher, and the learner him- or herself are all critical to any individual student's success.

Research seems to support the idea that technology can enhance the quality of student writing. Several studies have shown that when students are using word-processing software, they make more revisions, write longer compositions, and have fewer errors in their final drafts. It is important, however, to note that students' ease and experience with the technology are critical variables. It is important to give children time to become comfortable with the computer and any software that is being used. Also, the ease with which the software can be used and the quality of the hardware (for example, if it operates too slowly for the student to progress at a reasonable rate) can affect student success.

Software programs offer a variety of features to support students' composing processes; and the teacher has a significant role in evaluating the software, not only for LD students as recommended by Lewis et al. (1996), but for all students. Teachers should themselves use software programs before asking their students to use them. Then the teacher can make suggestions to individual students regarding what is likely to be helpful and what may potentially be problematic.

Another important role for the teacher is to arrange the classroom in a way that will make the best use of computers for writing. For example, children should not become isolated from their peers when they are composing at a computer. The room should be arranged so that collaboration is not compromised. There is some evidence that students do even more collaborating when they are writing at the computer. Therefore, the classroom can be arranged to encourage peer discussions and feedback regarding their writing.

Finally, worth mentioning is the fact that the optimum writing environment might include both "high technology" (computers and word processing) and "low technology" (pen, paper, and pencil). Keeping pen and paper available might offer students more flexibility for thinking and planning both before and during writing. There is evidence that computers without special planning features limit students' planning to the novice stage in which the preliminary notetaking and eventual text are one and the same. Also, it might be useful to encourage students to print out their drafts-in-progress periodically because the computer screen can limit a writer's ability to step back from a text and reconsider it beyond the text captured only on the screen at any given moment.

It seems clear that technology can enhance students' writing proficiency. As with any instructional process, we must monitor students' progress and evaluate the impact on learning. Although there is research to inform us regarding the use of technology in writing, many questions remain to be answered. We discuss some of those questions in the next section of this chapter.

Looking Ahead

There are those who urge that educators exercise caution in the accelerating rush toward technology. For example, O'Neil (1996) reported several interesting perspectives drawn from his interviews with Crawford Kilian, a novelist and teacher in British Columbia, and Clifford Stoll, a long-time computer user and author who has written extensively about the Internet. Stoll, in his interview, cautioned that we must be certain that technology in a learning environment actually supports the learning. He commented that "people are rushing in, quite blindly, to promote computers for reasons that have little to do with education" (O'Neil, 1996, p. 14). As an example, he talks about the excitement that teachers exude when talking about research their students are conducting over the Internet. Although students may enjoy using the computer, he argues that research over the Internet is not necessarily better or more useful than research done with textbooks. If fact, if students merely search the Internet for information, which they then cut and paste into their own papers, they will have done the opposite of quality research, which involves the hard work of analyzing, synthesizing, and reflecting on ideas and information.

In his interview with O'Neil, Kilian expresses the need to consider what we give up when we immerse ourselves in an online environment. As an example, he states:

> In the online environment, you definitely miss a lot of what goes on in a classroom. It's as if you were an opera performer and I tried to coach you over the phone. I can hear you singing, perhaps, but I would miss most of the overtones and undertones because the bandwidth is so narrow. (p. 16)

A similar caution comes from Selfe (1992), who writes about the importance of preparing teachers to use technology effectively for teaching and learning. She writes that we will be making a "bad trade" if we "let concerns about bits and bytes, computer-assisted instruction and computer-managed instruction, RAM and ROM eclipse our larger vision of humanist concerns as we educate teachers to design and implement and teach within virtual environments" (p. 38). What specifically is she concerned about? She urges that we, as educators, not give up the priority that "places people, their feelings, their impressions and interpretations of life, the study of human experience and the written expressions about this experience at the center of our attention" (p. 38).

In addition to this concern, there are many others that arise out of what we are learning about technology and writing. For example, it is important that an increasing rush to technology be mediated by serious attempts to answer questions and address concerns that emerge when technology, writing, and goals for learning intersect.

One issue that must be dealt with is knowing that computer software, rather than being simply a tool for writing, has the power to influence our thinking about writing. The software has potential for affecting the way we approach writing—the processes we use when we write and how we use them. As we increasingly use technology for writing, questions that must be asked and answered include the following: To what degree do software programs affect an individual's thinking about writing? And how? Might such programs not only facilitate composition, but also influence mental processes associated with making meaning and producing text? What processes and procedures are privileged by some software programs and not others? For example, do particular CAC programs focus on a cognitive approach to writing, emphasizing processes, procedures, and information, while ignoring the role of social interaction in composition processes? Might some CAC programs, as well as the hardware itself, actually interfere with writing?

Another important question about technology and writing relates to how the teacher's role changes in a technological writing environment. There are certainly multiple answers to that question, all of which depend on the technologies being used. What new knowledge does the teacher need? How do student-teacher and student-student interactions change? What classroom designs best facilitate writing development when students are using word processing or other CAC programs? What instructional practices best allow students to thrive as writers working with word-processing software, and how do these practices differ across a spectrum of students' ages and abilities?

The potential for questioning is large. What is the role of parents and the community in supporting technology's role in writing and learning? How can teachers become partners in this endeavor? That question, brings up issues of access for all students and the communities in which they live. What is the role of the university and teacher-preparation programs in instructing teachers how to support literacy development in technological environments? What knowledge regarding technology and learning should preservice teachers take into their profession, so that they will be ready and able to contribute productively to the integration of technology and writing?

To investigate these issues, research must center on relations between technology implementation and educational knowledge that is based in learning theory, composition theory, curriculum goals, and issues of classroom diversity. We believe there is an urgent call, based on a critical need to know, for classroom action research, for districtwide research, and for collaborations among K–12 and university teachers to conduct research and disseminate findings that can add to the knowledge base of the entire educational community regarding technology and learning, particularly in the area of writing.

CHAPTER 7

Research on Assessment in Writing

The fundamental purpose of writing assessment is learning—learning about what works in a writing task and what represents quality. Spandel and Stiggins (1997) make what we believe is a very important statement about assessment in writing, that "assessment—good assessment—has very little to do with grades" (p. 23). This chapter explores various types of writing assessment and what they show us about writing instruction.

Although the purpose of this chapter is not to review the variety of useful texts that are available, many useful books and articles have been written about assessment in writing. In addition to those that are mentioned in the context of the research discussed in this chapter, there are several others that we would like to note because we have found them particularly useful. They include *Portfolio Assessment in the Reading-Writing Classroom* by Tierney, Carter, and Desai (1991); Harp's *Assessment and Evaluation for Student Centered Learning* (1994); and Rhodes and Shanklin's *Windows Into Literacy: Assessing Learners K–8* (1993). And certainly there are other texts, besides those and others mentioned in this chapter, that offer important insights regarding writing assessment.

Forms of Writing Assessment

Indirect Versus Direct Assessment

Over the past decade, large-scale writing assessments have changed from using multiple-choice tests, which, although simple to administer and easy to score, offer very little in the way of understanding how writers do such things as express their ideas, present a rationale to create a compelling argument, or organize their thoughts around evidence to support a premise. These multiple-choice tests offered indirect documentation of writing performance, where writing quality had to be inferred from students' abilities to correct spelling errors, find errors in capitalization and punctuation, and distinguish sentences from nonsentences.

Today, large-scale writing assessments assess writing directly by providing prompts in response to which students actually write. Spandel and Stiggins (1997) describe several benefits of these large-scale, direct writing assessments. One benefit is that these assessments and their results keep the importance of writing in front of the public. They also provide motivation for educators to develop increasingly valid and consistent scoring criteria and processes. In addition, teachers who take part in the scoring of large-scale assessments have opportunities to read a wide range of students' writings beyond their own classrooms. However, as Spandel and Stiggins note, the most important contribution of these assessments is that they have raised expectations about student performance. Direct writing assessments provide profiles of what students (for example, fourth-grade writers) are doing well in their writing, as well as what difficulties need to be addressed in schools and classrooms. Through direct assessment, educators can learn about the strengths evident in the compositions of young writers and can then, based on the information, plan directions for the writing curriculum and organize specific instruction. Although critics point out that large-scale assessments do not provide individual student scores and, most often, represent results from only first-draft writing, they nonetheless provide a much more useful profile of student writing than the indirect method of a multiple-choice test (Spandel & Stiggins, 1997).

Three Types of Direct Assessment

There are three frequently used forms of direct assessment: primary trait, holistic, and analytic scoring. *Primary trait* scoring is not very useful for large-scale assessments because it focuses on only one trait, the one that, depending on the purpose for a writing, represents its defining characteristic. For example, in a report of information the primary trait or characteristic would be sufficient elaboration of information centering on a question or topic. If the purpose is to provide information, then elaboration would be the writing's primary trait. In a classroom, this type of scoring might be useful as a way to help teachers and young writers identify whether the primary purpose of a writing had been met.

Holistic scoring, on the other hand, assesses writing based on a general impression, usually represented by a single score. For instance, in order to receive a score of six on a six-point holistic rubric, a report of information would have to address a specific topic or question, clearly provide relevant and significant information in a logical and coherent manner that engages the reader, and include very few errors in conventions (for example, spelling, syntax, capitalization, and punctuation) and only those that even experienced writers might make. Receiving a six on this rubric indicates a writing of very high quality, and although receiving a three would indicate that a writer's report of information were of lesser quality, there is no way of explicitly knowing the writer's strengths and problems. Although a holistic score can be useful to provide a snapshot of writing achievement, its flaw is that it provides little information that can be used to plan and develop subsequent instruction.

Analytic assessment, unlike holistic general impression scoring, looks at multiple elements or characteristics associated with effective writing. Of the three types of direct writing assessment, it provides the most information from which to draw conclusions about writers and writings. The elements must be selected according to the criterion that are directly relevant to quality in writing. There is no magic number and no magic list, although Spandel and Stiggins (1997) suggest six traits or elements that characterize effective writing: ideas, organization, voice, word choice, sentence fluency, and conventions. As an assessment system, analytic scoring offers information that can best assist instruction because each element in a writing is evaluated separately, with each characteristic marked on a scale that indicates how well it has been presented. For example, an exceptionally well-organized writing may receive a score of six for organization but a score of three for sentence fluency if its sentences are choppy, lengthy and convoluted, or full of ambiguity.

Although a discussion of various assessment systems is useful and informative to those who are interested in writing development, our purpose here is to focus on what research tells us about writing assessments. We begin with one of the more recent assessment processes to be used in writing—the portfolio. We then move to a discussion of the effects of rubrics on writing assessment; and, finally, we examine what research tells us about a traditional form of assessment—the evaluation of writing based on elements of grammar, punctuation, and capitalization. (Although writing conferences are closely linked to assessment in writing, research on conferences is discussed in depth in Chapter 3 of this book.)

Portfolio Assessment

Definitions of Writing Portfolios

Portfolios are receiving increasing attention as vehicles for writing assessment. They are designed to collect and organize materials, provide a vehicle for evaluation and assessment, promote self-reflection, and document both processes and products. Paulsen and Paulsen (1994) offer a definition of a portfolio as a purposeful, integrated collection of student work that shows student effort, progress, or achievement in one or more areas. The collection includes evidence of student self-reflection and student participation in setting the focus, establishing the standards, selecting content, and judging merit (p. 2). This definition is useful because it speaks directly to the fundamental purposes for portfolio assessment, which include supporting instruction and bringing assessments in line with curriculum (Salinger & Chittenden, 1994). Portfolio assessment allows teachers to monitor student progress over time based on a collection of evidence, subsequently to be used for instructional planning and for providing feedback to developing writers.

Camp (1993) describes various portfolio systems in terms of a continuum. On one end are portfolios that are very test-like. They contain student samples, selected either by the student or the teacher (or both); written reflections are attached to each work for the purpose of garnering students' thoughts about content and process associated with a particular piece. Although such portfolios encourage reflection, they are also highly standardized. At the other end of the continuum are portfolios that not only attempt to assess student learning, but also guide instruction, encourage reflection, and support learning. These portfolios may contain works in various degrees of completion, and the instructional processes that are used with the portfolios encourage self-reflection, as well as regular feedback from peers, teachers, and parents. Although these portfolios may be used to assess student writing, they are usually evaluated with guidelines and rubrics designed jointly by students and teachers, and the evaluations tend to focus on assessment of ongoing student learning and development and to be narrative rather than numerical.

Research on Portfolio Assessment

Much information on the use of portfolios for assessment in writing has been anecdotal, consisting primarily of descriptions of various portfolio models and their use. Although portfolios have been touted as a contextualized and authentic assessment that not only serve as a measure of learner progress and achievement, but also support ongoing learning, evidence regarding the effects of portfolios in these areas has emerged only relatively recently. Herman and Winters (1994) confirm this in their review of the 89 entries on portfolios that they found in the educational literature over the past 10 years. They report finding only seven articles that contained actual data regarding the quality of portfolios and effects of their use. Of those seven, several had to do with the technical quality of portfolios, particularly their reliability and validity.

Although some educators do not believe it is necessary to emphasize the reliability and validity of portfolios, Herman and Winters (1994) note that the value of portfolios outside of single classrooms is severely compromised if those qualities are not considered. The question of reliability relates both to students and to evaluators of their portfolios. Outside of the work collected in a portfolio, do students score similarly on tasks that are like those in the portfolios? If not, can the portfolio be considered a reliable indicator of student progress and achievement? Another important reliability question relates to whether evaluators of portfolios agree on their assessments. If, for example, two raters or evaluators assess a portfolio and its contents differently, then the scores may say more about the raters than they do about the student work being evaluated. Such scores cannot then be reported as indicators of anything more than rater disagreement.

Herman and Winter report on research from various school districts across the United States and the variability that exists in rater reliability. They conclude that several factors can be associated with helping to ensure a high degree of reliability among raters. These factors include the following:

- specific and clear criteria associated with portfolio development and evaluation,
- time allotted for effective training on portfolio development and scoring,
- use of guidelines or rubrics that represent shared understandings and values, and
- evaluators with expert's understanding of student performance.

Herman and Winter found that in districts with successful portfolio programs—that is, where ratings could be considered reliable indicators of student work—a high degree of collaboration among teacher raters was a necessary foundation for these factors.

Another issue that underlies the quality of a portfolio system is its validity. When portfolios are used as tools for assessment, do they assess what we think they are assessing? Are they trustworthy indicators of what we want to measure and what we think we are measuring? One way to determine validity is to see whether student achievement, as measured by other indicators of a particular performance, is similar to the results of portfolio assessment. This is difficult because multiple good indicators of a particular capability may be hard to find.

Nevertheless, it is important to establish in some way that portfolios are capturing the learning and the meanings that are being assessed. For example, what indicators of quality writing can be used comparatively with the results of writing portfolio assessments? Herman and Winters (1994) cite the work of Koretz and colleagues, who examined score relations between writing portfolio scores and direct writing assessment scores in Vermont. They found a weak to moderate correlation between the two. Unfortunately, this is not a particularly good indicator that the writing portfolios and the direct writing assessment were evaluating the same thing.

The research of Gearhart and her colleagues, through the National Center for Research on Evaluation, Standards, and Student Testing (CRESST), offers another interesting perspective on the validity of portfolios (Gearhart, Herman, Baker, & Whittaker, 1992). They found almost no relation between ratings of writing portfolios and students' results on a standardized writing assessment. In addition, they discovered that when portfolios were scored two different ways—one a holistic score for the portfolio and one an averaged score based on individual works in the same portfolio—half of students who would be classified as "masters" based on the one score would not have been so classified based on the averaged score from the individual pieces. The portfolios tended to be scored higher. This raises a major question: How does one trust whether portfolios actually assess what they purport to measure? Do they underestimate or overestimate student performance? An important issue to consider is whether the support and collaboration that students receive in the development of their portfolios lead to a level of achievement not seen when students work on their own.

Gearhart and her colleagues also discovered that a high degree of rater agreement could be achieved, using holistic ratings, to assess portfolio collections. The teachers conducting the assessments were familiar with the scoring guides and worked together to establish a high level of agreement using "training samples" of student work. However, the teachers raised questions regarding the use of portfolios for large-scale assessments. Although they did not absolutely rule this out, they expressed concerns that, first of all, the portfolios would have to be structured to match the objectives of the assessment. They also noted that raters should be aware of teachers' expectations for students' performance in the portfolios, that raters should have access to the descriptions of assignments and writing tasks, and that they should be aware of the degree to which a student may have had assistance with work in the portfolio.

THE KEEP PROGRAM. Results from large portfolio projects offer additional insights for the development of portfolio systems. Au (1994) describes the Kamehameha Elementary Education Program (KEEP) and its use of portfolios for program evaluation. This portfolio system was oriented to collection of writing samples which were stipulated by the district personnel. There was little student involvement or student-teacher collaboration on portfolio contents. In retrospect, Au reported several concerns that arose from this project: more student involvement might have helped students feel a sense of ownership of the process, there was a lack of perceived connection for many teachers between the literacy curriculum and the portfolio system, and teachers often felt unprepared to make the professional judgments necessary to infer instructional and program implications from the portfolios.

THE BELLEVUE LITERACY ASSESSMENT PROJECT. In their description of the Bellevue Literacy Assessment Project, Valencia and Place (1994) report on a complex portfolio system that included showcasing student work in the following ways:

- work that students chose for their portfolios;
- work that was specified by teachers and that was scored to monitor student progress and achievement;
- work that was placed in the portfolio to provide documentation of literacy levels, without necessarily being assessed according to specific scoring criteria; and
- multiple drafts of compositions that highlighted ongoing progress.

Valencia and Place discuss several insights from this research. They discovered that not all portfolios were consistent in the kinds of works they included, thereby affecting the conclusions that could be made regarding what was assessed. They also reported that some students resisted the use of portfolios when they were required to complete entry forms for certain pieces of writing.

THE RHODE ISLAND LITERACY PORTFOLIO ASSESSMENT PROJECT. Other insights come from Snider, Lima, and DeVito's (1994) research on the Rhode Island Literacy Portfolio Assessment Project. This is the most student centered of the three large projects described here. Two particular findings stand out. One was that clear goals and criteria for desired student outcomes must be made explicit for both students and teachers. Only in this way could they confidently assess whether the portfolios captured the quality of student achievement. A second finding centered on the importance of student-teacher collaboration on items selected for the portfolios. By modeling how such decisions for inclusion might be made, teachers worked with students who had primary responsibility for item selection to ensure that their selections were representative of student achievement.

JOHNSON'S COMPARATIVE RESEARCH. Although much of the research described in this section regarding portfolios has focused on the quality of the portfolio system itself, one middle-school teacher researcher (Johnson, 1995) was interested in the effects of different portfolio designs on eighth-grade students' attitudes toward writing. His school implemented a rather formalized, teacher-created portfolio system consisting of a checksheet to document contents and a table of contents. In addition, each portfolio was required to have at least one writing sample for each of eight writing types (for example, story, autobiographical incident, report of information, observational writing, and evaluation essay) and at least one piece through which the student could display evidence of progress.

Working with his school, Johnson received permission to use the schoolwide portfolio in one class and a slightly modified version of this portfolio system, modeled after the New Standards Project 94, in another class. This project, directed out of the National Center on Education and the Economy and funded by membership dues and grants, was begun in 1990 as a coalition of school districts and states for the purpose of developing, piloting, and eventually disseminating, standards and portfolio assessments in math and language arts. In 1994, the middle school portfolio project was being piloted in school districts around the country, and it was this portfolio system which Johnson adapted for use with his treatment group.

Both classes were heterogeneously grouped and were similar in age, ability, gender, and ethnicity. The modified portfolio design offered more emphasis on student selection and, although it required that certain writing types be included, those types of writing were defined on the basis of function (for example, writing as a guide to action, persuasive writing, response to literature, telling a story) as opposed to type (for example, biographical sketch, story, evaluation essay, report of information). What this meant was that an essay, rather than being narrowly defined as an evaluation essay, could have been written to fulfill more than one writing function. Students could write an essay to persuade or as a guide to action. Similarly, they could have told a story to persuade or present a response to literature. The functions and purposes of writing were highlighted rather than an emphasis on narrowly defined types of writing.

The curriculum was identical in both classes, and students' responses to a writing attitude survey, administered at the beginning of the school year, showed no significant differences. In contrast, the same survey, administered toward the end of the academic year, yielded some striking differences. Students in the modified portfolio class showed significantly more positive attitudes toward both essay and story writing. They were more inclined to take risks and try new things in their writings. Perhaps both of these findings may be attributed to the fact that the modified portfolio was more oriented toward the function and purposefulness of writing. There was also more flexibility in that students could decide for themselves what kind of writing best fulfilled for them a particular purpose. As the researcher commented, "The requirements were worded in such a way that directed students to accomplish something more than just following a form" (Johnson, 1995, p. 40).

The modified portfolio group evidenced, in comparing the pre- and postsurvey, increasingly positive attitudes toward editing and revision, as did the control group that used the schoolwide portfolio system. However, although the postsurvey difference between the two groups was not statistically significant, attitudes of the treatment group that used the modified-design portfolio showed a more dramatic change toward the positive than did the control group. Perhaps, again, students' attitudes were more positive toward revision and editing because they were working with a more flexible, function-oriented, and student-centered portfolio system.

Johnson found that students working with the modified portfolio system were generally more positive about maintaining a portfolio. Their comments centered on an appreciation of reflection and of the portfolio as a way to monitor their writing. Overall, they did not find the portfolio process tedious or burdensome. On the other hand, the control class reported that they had difficulty choosing their best works for the portfolio, a feeling that was compounded by their reporting that at times their best works were not on the required list of portfolio selections. Overall, they tended to find the process difficult and confusing.

Questions remain regarding how to ensure that writing portfolios are both valid and reliable and that they provide not only a way to assess writing, but also an effective support for students' growth and development as writers. In the next section of this chapter we discuss research on another assessment system, rubrics, designed to support writing development and inform instruction.

The Relation Between Standards for Writing and Writing Assessment

In Chapter 1 we discussed the difficulty that writers, particularly novice writers, have with revision when they do not have specified standards or criteria and clear intentions in relation to a particular writing. The problem is that when writers lack specific standards and intentions, their ability to reflect on and evaluate their writing is severely compromised. It is not surprising that if writers do not know what they want to accomplish with a particular writing, it will be difficult for them to judge whether they have created an effective composition. In this section of the chapter we examine the relations among the following: the setting of standards and criteria for a particular writing, a writer's ability to evaluate his own or someone else's writing, and overall writing quality. We turn to the work of two teacher researchers whose work provides some insights.

Sperling's Research: Establishing Standards

Sperling (1993) reports on the classroom research of Gail Hughes, a fourth-grade teacher who was disappointed that, in spite of using portfolios for student writing and giving students regular feedback on their writings, her students' writing showed little or no improvement. Sperling, who worked with Hughes and other teachers as the district's classroom assessment specialist, noticed that Hughes often evaluated similar student papers quite differently and that, when asked, she had difficulty articulating the criteria she used in the evaluations.

This difficulty is similar to the pattern documented in research on writing evaluation. Stiggins (1988) reported in his summary of 10 years of research that teachers spend at least 25% of each day assessing students, but that their criteria for assessing were seldom articulated. Although teachers had their own sense of how they were evaluating student work, their criteria were often implicit and not clearly formulated. As a result of this finding, Stiggins urged teachers to make their criteria explicit, not only for themselves but for their students, as well (Spandel & Stiggins, 1997).

In her fourth-grade classroom, Hughes began to develop specific criteria for what she wanted students to achieve in their writing. She also involved her students in this process. As the criteria developed, she and her students also created examples that helped further clarify the criteria. For example, students often used the word *interesting* as a criterion for evaluating sentences. Together, Hughes and her students fleshed out this concept by tying to the criterion such attributes as humor, personal opinion, colorful adjectives, similes, personal observations, and sound of the author's voice. Hughes then provided models of writing that might meet the criterion of *interesting*.

After developing a list of criteria, Hughes created an assessment form that described a continuum of quality in students' writing. This continuum contained criteria describing what represented high-quality writing, as well as poor writing, so that students would be aware of not only what the writing should look like, but also what it should not look like. Students used criteria on the assessment form to compare their evaluations with those of the teacher, and they collaborated with their peers to discuss their evaluations of writings.

A major finding from Sperling's (1993) teacher-research project was that students in Hughes's class all accomplished the fourth-grade writing outcomes and that the most improvement was found among the lowest achieving students. In their self-reports, students credited the collaborative assessments as having the greatest impact on their ability to think critically about their writing.

Boyle's Research: Rubric Training

Teacher researcher Cathy Boyle (1996), also working with fourth graders, was concerned with her students' struggles to create effective persuasive writings. Although their struggles mirrored results of the 1992 U.S. National Assessment of Educational Progress's Writing Report Card, which reported that only 20% of students performed at adequate or above levels in presenting and supporting a point of view, Boyle hypothesized that an instructional intervention might produce different results. She hypothesized that if students better understood the criteria for persuasive writing, presented in the form of scoring rubrics, they would be better able to compose more effective persuasive writings. She wondered whether training in rubric scoring, specifically for persuasive writing, would affect student writing. She was also interested in analyzing differences and similarities between teacher evaluations and student evaluations when both were using the same rubrics for assessment.

Boyle conducted her research in two fourth-grade classrooms with similar student groupings. Each class was comprised of students of high, average, and low academic ability. Both classrooms used the same writing curriculum in which both wrote five persuasive compositions, with the first and fifth serving as pre- and postsamples for Boyle's research. In the treatment classroom, students collaborated with their teacher in the development and use of holistic scoring rubrics for persuasive writing. Holistic scoring was used to evaluate students' writings against common standards (based on certain criteria) found in exemplary writings. (For additional readings about holistic scoring, as well as other scoring systems, there are several useful texts available. Two of those are Bratcher's *Evaluating Children's Writing* [1994] and Spandel & Stiggins's *Creating Writers: Linking Writing Assessment and Instruction* [1997].) As the rubric was being developed, student writings were reviewed, scored, and rewritten. Students also participated in peer evaluation sessions, which often were followed by rewriting sessions in which revisions were informed by peer feedback.

In the control classroom, students received teacher feedback, both written and verbal, on their writing, and participated in individual student-teacher writing conferences. Students in this classroom also participated in rewriting sessions, during which they considered the feedback they received from their teacher.

Boyle's findings revealed significant differences between the two groups. Based on scoring of the presamples, the two classrooms began this study at somewhat different levels of proficiency regarding persuasive writing. The mean score on a six-point rubric was 2.5 for the control class; in the treatment class the mean score was 2.0. On the postsample, the 27 students in the treatment class had a mean score of 3.11, which represents a statistically significant change from the pre- to postwriting. In the control class, the mean postsample score was 2.5, identical to the mean presample score, showing no growth from the pre- to postwriting sample. It appears that students who participated in developing scoring rubrics and who learned to use them in self- and peer evaluations became more proficient writers of persuasive essays.

An interesting finding from this research was that when results of scoring by students in the treatment class were compared with teachers' scoring of those same writings, 83% of the papers evaluated by students were considered the same as the teacher-evaluated samples. Student and teacher scores were considered the same when the student-scored samples were given exactly the same scores as the teacher evaluators, or when they were within one point of each other. Not only did students' writing improve as a result of creating and using scoring rubrics for persuasive writing, over 80% of the students' peer evaluations aligned with teachers' evaluations.

In contrast to the treatment group, the control group did not show significant improvement in their writing when writing assessment was conducted through traditional means of teacher grades, teacher comments on written work, and student-teacher conferences. Similar to what Sperling found in the study described earlier, Boyle concluded that when students think critically about and develop standards for writing, and when they are able to evaluate writing according to the standards collectively set by teachers and students, they will develop as writers. In both studies, students and teachers worked together to review what areas of a writing needed improvement and then set goals or criteria to meet those standards. For both Hughes's class and Boyle's treatment group, this was a continuous process of improvement through defining, evaluating, and refining the standards.

Based on interviews with her students, Boyle also discovered that students believed that they learned to be more conscientious about appropriate use of conventions in their own writing as a result of evaluating the work of their peers. They commented that the rubrics helped them see errors in their peers' writings, and also helped them relate those findings to their own writings, where they became better evaluators of their own use of conventions. They were also better able to judge when critical elements of persuasive writing were missing from their essays. Boyle concluded that key factors in writing development include a clear definition of standards, which in her research was exemplified in collaborative rubric development and the experience of using rubrics to evaluate many writing samples.

Research on Holistic Evaluation

Boyle's work with rubrics and their development, described in the previous section, involved holistic evaluation. Cooper, in his introduction to the text *Evaluating Writing: Describing, Measuring, Judging* (Cooper & Odell, 1977), defines holistic evaluation as a guided procedure for sorting or ranking written pieces. The rater takes a piece of writing and does one of the following actions:

1. matches it with another piece in a graded series of pieces,
2. scores it for the prominence of certain features important to that kind of writing, or
3. assigns it a letter or number grade. (p. 3)

Boyle's research was designed as it was partly because of information that has accrued from past research findings on writing assessment. A crucial element of her study involved ensuring that the raters, both student raters and teachers, were carefully trained in using the holistic scoring guides.

Cooper and Odell (1977) presented a review of research that showed that the reliability of holistic evaluation can be questionable. In general, it was well established through a line of research that began over 60 years ago that, given a particular essay, a group of raters, even raters who are experienced teachers, will evaluate it with widely differing scores. The problem with this is that the scoring cannot be considered reliable when no two scores on an essay are the same, because the scoring then says more about the rater than the writing itself. Cooper (1977) also points out that research offers strong evidence to the effect that scoring can become reliable "when raters from similar backgrounds are carefully trained" (p. 18).

In fact, he cites research from 1934 in which rater reliability on the scoring of writing could be increased "from a range of .30 to .75 before training to a range of .73 to .98 after training" (p. 18). He explains that the higher coefficients are generally considered high enough to be considered reliable for program evaluation, and that at the .90 level are considered reliable enough to be considered useful in reporting individual growth in writing.

As a result of his research review, Cooper emphasizes certain elements that must be in place if holistic assessment of writing can be considered reliable, two of which are time and cooperation. Raters must have training that involves the experience of scoring many papers, and they must collaborate with other raters who have similar background and expertise in order to achieve a shared sense of how the scoring criteria are applied to different writings. Also, in order to have a reliable assessment of individual writers, Cooper recommends that at least two papers from each writer be scored. Because writers can vary greatly in their performance, two measures of a writer's achievement are more likely to offer a reliable picture of that writer's proficiency.

Although holistic scoring guides often include evaluation of a writer's use of mechanics in writing, the mechanics represent only one element to consider. It is not uncommon, however, that, without clear guidelines for scoring a writing and without training in the use of those guidelines, writing assessment often focuses primarily on issues related to grammar, punctuation, and capitalization.

Assessment of Grammar, Punctuation, and Capitalization

Performance in the mechanics of writing has often been considered an indicator of quality. Teachers struggle with the extent to which errors associated with grammar, spelling, punctuation, and capitalization should be judged as compromising writing quality. When do errors compromise the quality of a writing, and when are they only errors that even experienced writers may inadvertently make, thus not necessarily affecting writing quality? A related question centers on which instructional processes best support developing writers' ability to use mechanical conventions of writing appropriately. This chapter is, however, not about instruction in mechanics, although research does inform us in this regard (see Hillocks's 1986 research summary for an overview); instead, we look at what research tells us about assessment when it places primary emphasis on mechanics in writing.

The research base is small, and the findings are directly related to research on the effects of various instructional strategies in grammar and mechanics on writing quality. Like much research in writing, a sizable portion of the research in this area was conducted primarily with older students. For example, Adams (1971) compared two instructional processes in twelfth-grade classrooms. In one classroom, writing instruction was approached more informally; freewriting and creativity were stressed more than grammar and mechanics. In the other classroom, a more formal style was used, and issues of grammar and mechanics were emphasized. As part of the assessment of student writings, every error in the compositions of the second group was marked, and papers were returned to students for correction. During the duration of the study, Adams found no gain in overall writing quality in the informal group. However, the group in which attention was riveted on every error experienced a large decrease in writing quality.

Research on instructional processes designed to teach grammar and mechanics has failed over the past two decades to find strong support for the impact of such lessons on writing quality (for more on this topic, see Goddin's work with third and seventh graders [1969]; Fry's work with middle-school students [1972]; and Elley, Barham, Lamb, & Wyllie [1976]). It appears that, similarly, assessment that emphasizes grammar and mechanics offers only one limited view of writing quality and does not, by itself, provide the feedback that results in a positive effect on writing quality.

Effects of Teacher Comment as Writing Assessment

If writing assessment that emphasizes the marking of mechanical errors does not contribute to writing improvement, what kinds of markings or comments do lead to improvement? We turn again to Hillocks's 1986 review of writing research, in which he reports on research conducted from the mid-1960s through the early 1980s. Overall, some distinct commonalties emerge from this extensive body of

127

work, which contains research on young writers from the elementary grades through young adults in college.

One finding that might be considered surprising is that teacher comments, written on student papers and intended to provide both assessment and instructive feedback, had very little impact on writing improvement. Much of the research on teacher comments examined differences between effects of positive and negative comments, and found virtually no difference in writing quality between groups that received positive comments (for example, "good ideas," "good sentences," "clear description") and those that received negative comments (for example, corrections of word choice, grammar, punctuation, and spelling). One difference between the two groups did, however, emerge from the research. Writers receiving negative comments often had more negative feelings about writing and about themselves as writers, and more often felt frustrated in their writing.

One other interesting finding was revealed. Across the studies, teacher comments often tended to be diffuse. That is, on a single essay, teachers tended to address a wide variety of issues and problems all at once: organization, spelling, punctuation, and word choice, among others. In contrast, when the comments were more focused, providing, for instance, both positive and corrective feedback on a specific issue (for example, use of description or structure), writing quality showed marked improvement. This effect was heightened when teachers designed instructional strategies that specifically targeted the corrective comments, and, additionally, when student revision accompanied the instruction.

Teacher comments on a particular essay might focus on the positive aspects of a writer's ability to provide reasons in support of an argument about the need for a television rating system. In addition, comments might focus on ways the writer might more effectively handle the presentation of her reasons; perhaps she needs to be more explicit or to elaborate on her rationale or to provide more than one reason or point in support of her argument. Related instruction might include analyzing model argumentative essays, discussing characteristics of effective persuasive essays, evaluating essays of other students, and working on a revision of the draft. Teachers' comments, it appears, can have a profound effect on student writing, as long as they are focused rather than diffuse, and as long as they are accompanied directly by instruction that includes student revision.

Classroom Implications and Ideas for Instruction

Several themes emerge from the research on assessment in writing, especially in the areas of portfolio assessment and holistic scoring systems. One theme is that collaboration and shared expertise lie at the heart of effective assessment processes. Collaborations must occur among teachers and among teachers and students if writing assessment is to be based on criteria and expectations that everyone understands. Not surprisingly, shared understandings, based on a foundation of common knowledge and a similar degree of expertise among those who are scoring and assessing, are critical when it comes to setting and using standards and criteria against which to evaluate the various aspects of effective writing. Without specific criteria and guidelines that are clearly understood by everyone involved in the assessment process, including the students, it would be impossible to trust the results as being either reliable or valid.

Another theme found throughout the research on assessment centers on the actual development of standards and criteria. It is important that young writers are able to recognize characteristics of effective writing, and also are able to distinguish it, based on specific criteria, from writing that is less effective. By using writing models, some of which may be generated by students themselves, and by taking part in classroom conversations about elements of effective writing, young writers are able to become increasingly discerning writers and evaluators of writing. Students and their teachers together can develop criteria on which to base their assessments of writing. Through this development, young writers are able to become increasingly astute evaluators of their own and others' writings.

A third theme, related to the first two, centers on the element of time—time for collaboration and for training. Time is crucial to the process of developing a shared pool of knowledge regarding characteristics of effective writing. For example, two characteristics of exemplary autobiographical writing might be that it has a beginning that immediately engages readers and that the importance or significance of the autobiographical incident for the writer is either directly stated or implied. However, an effective beginning can take various forms, from relating a brief story or anecdote to describing a setting relevant to the autobiography. When evaluating autobiographical writings, teachers (and students) must have a common view of how these characteristics can appear within a certain kind of writing. This takes time.

In the area of portfolio development, it seems critical that teachers and students have clearly articulated and shared goals for portfolio use. As repositories of student writing, portfolios offer opportunities to support student reflection and growth in writing, in addition to providing a vehicle for broader assessment goals. Whatever portfolio format or system is used, it is important that students do not feel disconnected from the process, viewing it as just one more school task to complete. They should feel that the portfolio has value for them and that it can help them reflect on their writing and develop their expertise and power as writers.

Another area of research has important implications for the classroom. Evidence suggests that when assessment of writing focuses primarily on grammar and mechanics, students' writing development is not served. The same seems to be true of general teacher comments written in the margins of student compositions. Although this does not mean that teachers should ignore problems in students' writings, it does appear that the way those comments are used is important. For example, when the comments target specific elements, as opposed to being very general statements about the writing, and when subsequent instruction directly addresses these elements, there is potential for positive impact to help students' writing improve. However, questions remain about how best to address problems in student writing. We will pose some of these questions in the next section of this chapter.

Looking Ahead

Looking at research in classrooms with students in intermediate grades and above, it seems that children can be involved effectively in setting standards and criteria for particular writings. Students who have opportunities to read and discuss examples of effective writing often are able to participate in setting standards for writing and are able to use those standards and criteria to evaluate their own and their peers' writings. What might the effect be of involving primary-grade students in the development and use of specific criteria for writing? What would the processes of criteria-setting and rubric development look like in first or second grade? Would the quality of students' writing be affected? If so, in what ways? Would they become increasing-ly proficient at self-evaluation, at evaluating the writing of others, and at giving feedback to their peers?

If portfolios are to be viable vehicles for writing assessment, it is important that evaluations be both reliable and valid. The element of time is clearly an important variable for reliability. Has sufficient time been committed to ensure that evaluations are based on shared un-derstandings? In other words, is the evaluation a reliable reflection of student progress and achievement, or is it only the result of the views of particular raters? Also, an important consideration is whether stu-dent scores are reliable across similar tasks. It is important to establish this aspect of reliability in order to be certain that portfolios reflect student progress and achievement, rather than simply a student's serendipitous performance.

It appears that we must find ways to link portfolio structures di-rectly to our purposes for assessment—to what teachers and children value in writing and what they believe is important to assess. Perhaps only then can we be confident that portfolios actually reflect student achievement. In the area of validity, one question remains: Do port-folios allow us to assess the skills and proficiencies we think we are assessing? Do they, for instance, document specific writing profi-ciencies, math abilities, or comprehension skills? One area of concern relates to the degree of teacher support and peer collaboration that might contribute to any one student's portfolio. For assessment pur-poses, it is important to know how much of a portfolio reflects the individual student's ability and how much reflects a team effort.

Another aspect of portfolios centers on students' attitudes and per-ceptions toward developing and maintaining a portfolio. There is work yet to be done to determine how various portfolio designs affect stu-dents' attitudes and their metacognitive abilities, as well as their writ-ing. Is one portfolio design more effective than another in supporting students' positive attitudes about writing and about themselves as writers, and does that design vary with a writer's age and level of proficiency? In addition, do students' attitudes and perceptions re-garding portfolios affect the degree to which portfolios can serve to support learning and performance? In attempting to answer these questions, what does evidence, collected from a variety of sources including student surveys and interviews, as well as observations of how students actually use their portfolios, reveal about the power of portfolios to affect student learning and to serve as reliable and valid tools for assessment?

Another fertile area of research in writing assessment centers on the development and use of rubrics. It appears in the small amount of research that has been conducted that there is promise in teacher-student collaborations around the development of rubrics for writing, and that when students are given opportunities to engage in the critical thinking required to set criteria for a writing and to evaluate writing samples according to the criteria, young writers gain in writing proficiency. They also become increasingly adept at applying the criteria to the writings of others. This research, however, has been quite limited, and it is important to explore the effect of these assessment processes across genres and across age levels. Does the effect of student participation in rubric development and use vary by age or grade level, by a writer's ability level, or with students' language background? What are the key factors of rubric development that most influence writing achievement? If such questions were explored, perhaps the information could be integrated into instructional processes that would help students better evaluate their own writing, and, as a consequence, become more proficient writers.

Research evidence suggests that when assessment of writing focuses on mechanics, students' writing development is not served. In what way can assessments effectively address mechanics as one element of writing quality? Although error counts can be used as a reportable measure of mechanical control, in the research that has been conducted they do not appear effective as support for learning and growth. Perhaps the reason is that students had no role in this assessment process. There was no collaboration in the design of the assessment, no cooperative standard setting, and no commitment of time for developing shared understandings about effective mechanical control in writing. In addition, in the studies conducted, there was not subsequent instruction that occurred in the context of students' own writing to specifically address the items assessed. Therefore, the question remains: How can assessment be used to promote students' increasing proficiency in the mechanical control aspects of writing?

Assessments in writing serve multiple roles. They report learner progress and, perhaps more importantly, they function as part of the feedback loop between new learnings and increasing expertise. Research in this area has definite implications for teaching and learning. It also raises important points of inquiry, which, as we look ahead, will be important for classroom teachers and university researchers to explore.

CHAPTER 8

Thinking Back, Looking Ahead

We close this book with a retrospective view of research on children's writing. Our intent across all the chapters has been to highlight key research topics and issues related to classroom writing programs. Along the way, two questions kept focusing the work: What do we know about children's writing? and Where are the gaps in our knowledge? In other words, what is it that we do not know?

A Review of the Research

In the Introduction we discussed two ideas that guided our thinking and writing. One was to make clear the potential connections between research and practice. For that reason, each chapter has a section that discusses classroom implications and provides supporting evidence. The second idea was to pose questions that would engage teachers in inquiry and action research and that might be useful as catalysts for school-university research collaborations. Furthermore, as we wrote the Looking Ahead section of each chapter, it was our hope that the questions we posed might reveal other topics and avenues of exploration.

Our purpose across the preceding seven chapters was to explore lines of inquiry related to what we considered important content areas regarding children's writing. In the exploration, as in all research, questions surfaced that revealed some gaps in the knowledge base. These questions are critical because they highlight the importance of additional research yet to be done.

Based on the research we have selected, it seems that educators know a great deal about children's writing and about teaching and learning as they relate to the writing classroom. For example, we know there are many ways of researching and thinking about writing processes, as we come to understand better the nature of writers' processes, this fact will have definite implications for writing instruction. Understanding these processes, however, involves realizing the complex and interactive nature of writing processes and their variability. Writing processes vary with the day, the genre, the topic, the writer's level of knowledge, and the purpose for writing. We are informed by classroom research, yet recognize that writing can be constrained by classroom contexts that limit individual goal setting and that do not allow young writers to experience the nature of their own writing processes.

When we look closely at the research that specifically examines children's composing processes, we see variation among learners. The way learners write changes across writing events according to their interpretations of specific writing tasks and their social aims. Although research often describes writing as a problem-solving activity, it is also an act of discovery—writers discover what they have to say and who they are as writers by writing, generating ideas, and listening to other writers. In classroom research, writing is portrayed as a social and cultural event as children work in one another's company and develop as writers.

Current studies on writing development include more than an examination of children's growing knowledge of the conventions of writing. These studies also present the image of children grappling with the world that they know, considering what they have to say, and experimenting with the forms and functions of written language. Research on the craft of writing has provided some additional developmental information. Planning emerges as an area of interest, particularly for adolescents. Research also indicates that younger children may not separate planning from text generation and may need to prepare to write in groups. Social interactions with other writers may help young writers think about plans and consider ways to organize their writing. Similarly, audience awareness also may emerge as an area of interest through such classroom activities as conferencing or through author's theater experiences in which audience participation in the writer's story provides immediate feedback to illustrate the needs of readers. These possibilities and other changes in writing classrooms suggest the need for additional research. Researchers have yet to explore how these and other key areas of the writer's craft develop in specific curricular contexts, such as in rich genre-focused units in which abundant reading experiences provide examples and structures for writing.

When we read studies about writing instruction, it is clear that the complexity of classroom writing programs and the nature of teachers' work during instruction is rarely the focus. We do not yet have descriptions of how teachers make their decisions as they teach writing. We do not know how they think about and manage writing programs for a wide range of learners. There are not sufficient investigations of instruction for writers who experience difficulty and are less proficient in the area of writing than their classmates. We do have studies that inform specific teaching practices, such as methods to meet with young writers and ways to vary these conferences, but teachers need a wider array of field-tested options to support their instruction. It would be useful to know more about what conferencing strategies teachers use for writers at various grade levels and to gain a sense of elementary-grade children's perspectives on teacher-student conferences. In addition, as children experience themed units that integrate subject areas, our need for research about writing as a tool for learning increases. Additional research about writing instruction that demonstrates strategies for writing in subject areas is also an urgent need.

Venturing into the area of writing and technology, we know that recognizing trends is difficult because of the swiftness with which changes occur. The technology itself is changing rapidly; as a result, the rate at which teachers "find, try, discard, rediscover, adopt, adapt, and use applications of information technology to improve teaching and learning" is also accelerating rapidly (Gilbert, 1996, p. 10). In fact, Gilbert cautions that these changes are "outpacing the availability of conclusive research results" (p. 10). His comments reinforce the importance of conducting future research that will continue to inform us about the role of technology in writing.

Based on previous research, we know that computers and word-processing software function as more than merely fancy electronic typewriters. There is evidence, for example, that computer-assisted composition software (CAC), which is designed specifically to facilitate composition processes, has the potential not only to facilitate, but also to alter writing processes. Writing thus is not simply carried out through the technology, but the technology actually influences and shapes the writing. In the case of children with learning disabilities, some computer software has been found to support their writing processes, but other software has been found to interfere.

Another example of the effect of computers on children's writing is seen in the fact that young writers' collaborations can be enhanced or frustrated, depending on how computers are used in the classroom, for example their arrangement. Although there is some evidence that the quality of writing increases with the use of technology, these results are mixed and seem to vary around such things as a child's level of writing expertise and his or her experience using a keyboard.

In yet another area of inquiry, one of the questions educators continually ask themselves about writing is whether children are writing increasingly well within writing-instruction programs. Researchers have written about various kinds of writing assessments, all of which respond to different objectives and purposes. For example, if we want to see whether students are becoming increasingly fluent writers, a simple word count is sufficient. However, if we want to do quick, general-impression scoring that addresses multiple aspects of writing, holistic scoring would be the assessment of choice. Large-scale, direct assessments of student writing tend to use holistic scoring and to provide information that applies to groups, not individuals. Large-scale assessments most often reflect rough-draft writing rather than thoughtfully constructed compositions drafted over time. However, depending on the purpose for the assessment, these data can provide useful, albeit broad-based, information about writing achievement.

Research suggests that portfolios can be useful for writing assessment, but there are some potential pitfalls to consider. For example, students' perceptions of ownership of a portfolio system seem to color their willingness to invest time and energy in its development. Also, a portfolio may not represent the actual quality of a student's writing, meaning that it is important to discern whether a portfolio reflects a student's actual work, or instead represents a student's work based on contributions from numerous feedback sessions and collaborations with others. In either case, before conducting assessments and drawing conclusions, teachers should be aware of the original purpose of the portfolio and how the system was designed.

Another interesting idea to explore is how assessment and instruction can be closely intertwined by engaging young writers in the development of criteria for a particular writing and, concurrently, in the development of a writing rubric. As children participate in rubric development and then have opportunities to work on their own writings in the context of specific criteria, they seem able to be critical readers of their own work. They also seem to become increasingly effective at giving feedback to their peers.

Research Agendas for the Future

As we reflect on the research sampled across various aspects of children's writing and the questions that arise within these areas, we also are aware of what has not been addressed. What, for instance, can we learn about relations that exist between writing and other media, such as writing and drama, or writing and the visual arts? What is the possible or potential nature of these relations and the impact on children's writing at various grade levels?

A question with relevance to an increasing number of teachers in the United States centers on how we can best support the writing development of students who are learning English as their second language. In what ways do their developmental patterns differ from children whose native language is English? How can teachers use culturally oriented discourse patterns to help English language learners learn to write across the genres?

And what about teacher preparation? Where and to what extent does the teaching of writing fit into programs of teacher preparation? Institutions that educate teachers operationalize the importance of various subjects through mandated courses. What do beginning teachers learn about children's writing and ways of teaching children to become increasingly effective writers? Although ongoing professional development is important, it seems that curriculum and pedagogy related to teaching writing would be critical knowledge for those beginning their careers in education.

Throughout the United States, schools respond to national, state, and local reading initiatives. In many cases, support is available for professional development that addresses emergent reading and writing in content areas. However, it is difficult to find national or statewide initiatives regarding writing proficiency. Too often writing is viewed as an add-on. Although much study has been done about reading-writing connections, we have yet to capitalize on the impact of reading on writing improvement, and the impact of writing on reading development.

In addition, there is research evidence, as well as a great deal of anecdotal reporting, that children are writing throughout the curriculum more today than ever before. There is, however, a difference between causing writing to occur and actually having a well-defined curriculum in which children are taught to improve their writing. Although fluency and frequency in writing are critical to writing development, they are not sufficient by themselves. What are the characteristics of classrooms where children consistently learn to improve their writing? For example, is a teacher's experience with writing a factor? For years, we (the authors of this book) have informally surveyed preservice and inservice teachers regarding their self-perceptions as readers and writers. Overwhelmingly, as a group, teachers see themselves as readers, but too often only a handful from any group reports a self-concept that includes being a writer. Although teaching methods may be important to support children's writing development, we think the teacher as writer is also a significant element in the success of classroom writing programs.

We contend that many areas of children's writing remain to be explored, and that there is much research ahead regarding the implications for curriculum and instruction. There are many conversations yet to be held and many ideas to be explored. We hope that this text contributes to the discussion.

References

Adams, V.A. (1971). *A study of the effects of two methods of teaching composition to twelfth graders*. Unpublished doctoral dissertation, University of Illinois, Champaign-Urbana.

Atwell, N. (1986). *In the middle: Writing, reading, and learning with adolescents*. Portsmouth, NH: Heinemann.

Atwell, N. (1990). *Coming to know: Writing to learn in the intermediate grades*. Portsmouth, NH: Heinemann.

Au, K.H. (1994). Portfolio assessment: Experiences at the Kamehameha Elementary Education Program. In S.W. Valencia, E.H. Heibert, & P.P. Afflerbach (Eds.), *Authentic reading assessment: Practices and possibilities* (pp. 103–133). Newark, DE: International Reading Association.

Avery, C. (1993). *...And with a light touch: Learning about reading, writing, and teaching with first graders*. Portsmouth, NH: Heinemann.

Bagge-Rynerson, B. (1994). Learning good lessons: Young readers respond to books. In T. Newkirk (Ed.), *Workshop 5: The writing process revisited* (pp. 90–100). Portsmouth, NH: Heinemann.

Bangert-Drowns, R.L. (1993). The word processor as an instructional tool: A meta-analysis of word processing in writing instruction. *Review of Educational Research, 63*, 69–93.

Bear, D., Invernizzi, M., Templeton, S., & Johnston, F. (1996). *Words their way: Word study for phonics, vocabulary, and spelling instruction*. Upper Saddle River, NJ: Prentice-Hall.

Beers, J., & Henderson, E. (1977). A study of developing orthographic concepts among first graders. *Research in the Teaching of English, 11*, 133–148.

Bereiter, C., & Scardamalia, M. (1987). *The psychology of written composition*. Hillsdale, NJ: Erlbaum.

Birnbaum, J. (1982). The reading and composing behavior of selected fourth- and seventh-grade students. *Research in the Teaching of English, 16*, 241–260.

Boyle, C. (1996). *Efficacy of peer evaluation and effects of peer evaluation on persuasive writing*. Unpublished master's thesis, San Diego State University, San Diego, CA.

Braddock, R., Lloyd-Jones, R., & Schoer, L. (1963). *Research in written composition*. Urbana, IL: National Council of Teachers of English.

Bratcher, S. (1994). *Evaluating children's writing: A handbook of communication choices for classroom teachers*. New York: St. Martin's Press.

Britton, J., Burgess, T., Martin, N., McLeod, A., & Rosen, H. (1975). *The development of writing abilities*. London: Macmillan Education.

Bruce, B., Michaels, S., & Watson-Gegeo, K. (1985). How computers change the writing process. *Language Arts, 62*, 143–149.

Burtis, P.J., Scardamalia, M., Bereiter, C., & Tetroe, J. (1983). The development of planning in writing. In B. Kross & G. Wells (Eds.), *Explorations in the development of writing* (pp. 153–174). London: Wiley.

Calkins, L.M. (1983). *Lessons from a child*. Portsmouth, NH: Heinemann.

Calkins, L.M. (1986). *The art of teaching writing*. Portsmouth, NH: Heinemann.

Calkins, L.M. (1994). *The art of teaching writing* (New Ed.). Portsmouth, NH: Heinemann.

Camp, R. (1993). The place of portfolios in our changing views of writing assessment. In R. Bennet & W. Ward (Eds.), *Construction versus choice in cognitive measurement: Issues in constructed response, performance testing, and portfolio assessment*. Hillsdale, NJ: Erlbaum.

Chapman, M. (1995). The sociocognitive construction of written genres in first grade. *Research in the Teaching of English, 29*, 164–191.

Cioffi, G. (1984). Observing composing behaviors of primary-age children: The interaction of oral and written language. In R. Beach & L.S. Bridwell (Eds.), *New directions in composition research* (pp. 171–190). New York: The Guilford Press.

Clarke, L. (1988). Invented versus traditional spelling in first graders' writings: Effects on learning to spell and read. *Research in the Teaching of English, 22*, 281–309.

Cochran-Smith, M. (1991). Word processing and writing in elementary classrooms: A critical review of related literature. *Review of Educational Research, 61*, 107–155.

Cochran-Smith, M., Kahn, J., & Paris, C.L. (1990). Writing with a felicitous tool. *Theory Into Practice, 29*, 235–247.

Cochran-Smith, M., & Lytle, S. (1993). *Inside/outside: Teacher research and knowledge*. New York: Teachers College Press.

Cochran-Smith, M., Paris, C.L., & Kahn, J.L. (1991). *Learning to write differently*. Norwood, NJ: Ablex.

Cooper, C.R. (1977). Holistic evaluation of writing. In C.R. Cooper & L. Odell (Eds.), *Evaluating writing: Describing, measuring, judging* (pp. 3–31). Urbana, IL: National Council of Teachers of English.

Cooper, C.R., & Odell, L. (Eds.). (1977). *Evaluating writing: Describing, measuring, judging.* Urbana, IL: National Council of Teachers of English.

Cooper, M., & Holzman, M. (1989). *Writing as social action.* Portsmouth, NH: Boynton/Cook.

Cordiero, P. (1988). Children's punctuation: An analysis of errors in period placement. *Research in the Teaching of English, 22,* 62–74.

Cordiero, P., Giacobbe, M., & Cazden, D. (1983). Apostrophes, quotation marks, and periods: Learning punctuation in the first grade. *Language Arts, 60,* 323–332.

Countryman, J. (1992). *Writing to learn mathematics: Strategies that work.* Portsmouth, NH: Heinemann.

Dahl, K., & Freppon, P. (1995). A comparison of innercity children's interpretations of reading and writing instruction in the early grades in skills-based and whole language classrooms. *Reading Research Quarterly, 31,* 50–75.

Daiute, C. (1986). Physical and cognitive factors in revising: Insights from studies with computers. *Research in the Teaching of English, 20,* 141–159.

Dickinson, D.K. (1986). Cooperation, collaboration and a computer: Integrating a computer into a first-second grade writing program. *Research in the Teaching of English, 20,* 357–378.

DiPardo, A., & Freedman, S. (1988). Peer response groups in the writing classroom: Theoretic foundations and new directions. *Review of Educational Research, 58,* 119–149.

Dyson, A.H. (1989). *Multiple worlds of child writers: Friends learning to write.* New York: Teachers College Press.

Dyson, A.H. (1991). Viewpoints: The word and the world—reconceptualizing written language development or, do rainbows mean a lot to little girls? *Research in the Teaching of English, 25,* 97–123.

Dyson, A.H. (1992). Whistle for Willie, lost puppies and cartoon dogs: The sociocultural dimensions of young children's composing. *Journal of Reading Behavior, 24*(4), 433–461.

Dyson, A.H. (1993a). *The social worlds of children learning to write in an urban primary school.* New York: Teachers College Press.

Dyson, A.H. (1993b). *From invention to social action in early childhood literacy: A reconceptualization through dialogue about difference* (Technical Rep. No. 67). Berkeley, CA: National Center for the Study of Writing.

Dyson, A.H. (1994). *The ninjas, the X-men, and the ladies: Playing with power and identity in an urban primary school* (Technical Rep. No. 70). Berkeley, CA: Center for the Study of Writing.

Dyson, A.H. (1995). Writing children: Reinventing the development of childhood literacy. *Written Communication, 12*, 4–46.

Dyson, A.H., & Freedman, S.W. (1991a). *Critical challenges for research on writing and literacy: 1990–1995* (Technical Rep. No. 1B). Berkeley, CA: Center for the Study of Writing.

Dyson, A.H., & Freedman, S.W. (1991b). Writing. In J. Flood, J.M. Jensen, D. Lapp, & J.R. Squire (Eds.), *Handbook of research on teaching the English language arts* (pp. 754–774). New York: Macmillan.

Eckhoff, B. (1983). How reading affects children's writing. *Language Arts, 60*, 607–616.

Elley, W.B., Barham, I.H., Lamb, H., & Wyllie, M. (1976). The role of grammar in a secondary school English curriculum. *Research in the Teaching of English, 10*, 5–21.

Emig, J. (1971). *The composing processes of twelfth graders*. Urbana, IL: National Council of Teachers of English.

Farnan, N., & Fearn, L. (1993). Writers workshops: Middle school writers and readers collaborating. *Middle School Journal, 24*, 61–65.

Finders, M. (1996). "Just girls": Literacy and allegiance in junior high school. *Written Communication, 13*, 93–129.

Fitzgerald, J. (1987). Research on revision in writing. *Review of Educational Research, 57*, 481–506.

Fitzgerald, J., & Markham, L.R. (1987). Teaching children about revision in writing. *Cognition and Instruction, 4*, 3–24.

Fitzgerald, J., & Stamm, C. (1992). Variation in writing conference influence on revision: Two cases. *Journal of Reading Behavior, 24*, 21–49.

Fletcher, R. (1993). *What a writer needs*. Portsmouth, NH: Heinemann.

Flower, L.S., & Hayes, J.R. (1980). Identifying the organization of writing processes. In L.W. Gregg & E.R. Steinberg (Eds.). *Cognitive processes in writing* (pp. 3–30). Hillsdale, NJ: Erlbaum.

Flower, L.S., & Hayes, J.R. (1981). A cognitive process theory of writing. *College Composition and Communication, 32*, 365–387.

Frank, L.A. (1992). Writing to be read: Young writers' ability to demonstrate audience awareness when evaluated by their readers. *Research in the Teaching of English, 26*(3), 277–298.

Fraser, J., & Skolnick, D. (1994). *On their way: Celebrating second graders as they read and write*. Portsmouth, NH: Heinemann.

Freedman, S.W., & Sperling, M. (1985). Written language acquisition: The role of response and the writing conference. In S.W. Freedman (Ed.), *The acquisition of written language: Response and revision* (pp. 307–315). Norwood, NJ: Ablex.

Fry, D.J.W. (1972). The effects of transformational grammar upon the writing performance of students of low socio-economic backgrounds. *Dissertation Abstracts International, 32*, 4835–A.

Gates, B. (1995). *The road ahead.* New York: Viking Press.

Gearhart, M., Herman, J.L., Baker, E.L., & Whittaker, A.K. (1992). *Writing portfolios: Potential for large-scale assessment.* Los Angeles, CA: National Center for Research on Evaluation, Standards, and Student Testing. (ERIC Document Reproduction Service No. ED 350 312)

Gentry, J., & Gillet, J. (1993). *Teaching kids to spell.* Portsmouth, NH: Heinemann.

Gere, A.R. & Abbot, R. (1985). Talking about writing: The language of writing groups. *Research in the Teaching of English, 19,* 362–381.

Gilbert, S.W. (March/April, 1996). Making the most of a slow revolution. *Change. 28,* 10–23.

Goddin, M.A.P. (1969). A comparison of the effect on student achievement of a generative approach and a traditional approach to the teaching of English grammar at grades three and seven. *Dissertation Abstracts International, 29,* 3522–A.

Goldstein, A.A., & Carr, P.G. (1996). *Can students benefit from process writing?* (NAEP facts, 1. Report No. NCES–96–845. ED 395 320). Washington, DC: U.S. Department of Education, National Center for Education Statistics.

Gordon, C.J., & MacInnis, D. (1993). Using journals as a window on students' thinking in mathematics. *Language Arts, 70,* 37–43.

Graves, D. (1975). The writing processes of seven-year-old children. *Research in the Teaching of English, 9,* 227–241.

Graves, D. (Ed.). (1981). *A case study observing the development of primary children's composing, spelling, and motor behaviors during the writing process* (Final report, NIE Grant No. G–78–0174. ED 218–653). Durham, NH: University of New Hampshire.

Graves, D. (1983). *Writing: Teachers and children at work.* Portsmouth, NH: Heinemann.

Graves, D. (1994). *A fresh look at writing.* Portsmouth, NH: Heinemann.

Gunnarsson, B.L. (1997). The writing process from a sociolinguistic viewpoint. *Written Communication, 14,* 139–188.

Haas, C. (1989a). Does the medium make a difference: Two studies of writing with computers. *Human Computer Interaction, 4,* 149–169.

Haas, C. (1989b). How the writing medium shapes the writing process: Effects of word processing on planning. *Research in the Teaching of English, 23,* 187–207.

Haas, C. (1989c). "Seeing it on the screen isn't really seeing it": Computer writers' reading problems. In G.E. Hawisher & C.L. Selfe (Eds.), *Critical perspectives on computers and composition instruction* (pp. 16–20). New York: Teachers College Press.

Haas, C. (1990). Composing in technological contexts: A study of note-making. *Written Communication, 7,* 512–547.

Hall, N. (1996). Learning about punctuation: An introduction and overview. In N. Hall & A. Robinson (Eds.), *Learning about punctuation.* Portsmouth, NH: Heinemann.

Hall, N., & Robinson, A. (Eds.). (1996). *Learning about punctuation.* Portsmouth, NH: Heinemann.

Hallenbeck, M.J. (1995). *The cognitive strategy in writing: Welcome relief for adolescents with learning disabilities.* Report presented at the Council for Exceptional Children Annual Convention (ED 381 981). Indianapolis, IN.

Hancock, M. (1993). Exploring the meaning-making process through the content of literature response journals: A case study investigation. *Research in the Teaching of English, 27,* 335–368.

Hansen, J. (1987). *When writers read.* Portsmouth, NH: Heinemann.

Harp, B. (Ed.). (1994). *Assessment and evaluation for student centered learning.* Norwood, MA: Christopher-Gordon.

Harper, K. (1997). *Composing as meaning-making: An examination of third-grade students' composing strategies and behaviors across curricular areas.* Unpublished doctoral dissertation, The Ohio State University, Columbus.

Harwayne, S. (1992). *Lasting impressions: Weaving literature into the writing workshop.* Portsmouth, NH: Heinemann.

Hawisher, G. (1986). Studies in word processing. *Computers and Composition, 4,* 6–31.

Herman, J.L., & Winters, L. (1994). Portfolio research: A slim collection. *Educational Leadership, 52,* 48–55.

Hillocks, G. (1986). *Research on written composition: New directions for teaching.* Urbana, IL: National Council of Teachers of English.

Hudson, S. (1986). Context and children's writing. *Research in the Teaching of English, 20,* 294–316.

Invernizzi, M., Abouzeid, M., & Gill, J.T. (1994). Using students' invented spellings as a guide for spelling instruction that emphasizes word study. *The Elementary School Journal, 95,* 155–167.

Jensen, J. (1993). What do we know about the writing of elementary school children? *Language Arts, 70,* 290–294.

Johnson, N.L. (1995). *The effect of portfolio design on student attitudes toward writing.* Unpublished master's thesis, San Diego State University, San Diego, CA.

Jones, I., & Pellegrini, A.D. (1996). The effects of social relationships, writing media, and microgenetic development of first-grade students' written narratives. *American Educational Research Journal, 33,* 691–718.

Kroll, B. (1985). Rewriting a complex story for a young reader: The development of audience-adapted writing skills. *Research in the Teaching of English, 19*(2), 120–139.

Kucer, S. (1985). The making of meaning. *Written Communication, 2,* 317–336.

Lane, B. (1993). *After the end: Teaching and learning creative revision.* Portsmouth, NH: Heinemann.

Langer, J. (1986a). *Children reading and writing: Structures and strategies.* Norwood, NJ: Ablex.

Langer, J. (1986b). Reading, writing, and understanding: An analysis of the construction of meaning. *Written Communication, 3,* 219–266.

Langer, J.A., & Applebee, A.N. (1987). *How writing shapes thinking.* Urbana, IL: National Council of Teachers of English.

LeBlanc, P. (1993). *Writing teachers/writing software: Creating our place in the electronic age.* Urbana, IL: National Council of Teachers of English.

Lensmire, T. (1994). *When children write: Critical re-visions of the writing workshop.* New York: Teachers College Press.

Lewis, R.B., Ashton, T., & Kieley, C. (1996). Word processing and individuals with learning disabilities: Overcoming the keyboard barrier. In *Eleventh Annual Conference of Technology for People with Disabilities* (pp.?). Northridge, CA: California State University.

Lloyd, P. (1987). *How writers write.* Portsmouth, NH: Heinemann.

Lyman, R.L. (1929). Summary of investigations relating to grammar, language, and composition. *Supplementary educational monographs, 36.* Chicago, IL: University of Chicago.

MacGillivray, L. (1994). Tacit shared understandings of a first-grade writing community. *Journal of Reading Behavior, 26*(3), 245–266.

Many, J., Fyfe, R., Lewis, G., & Mitchell, E. (1996). Traversing the topical landscape: Exploring students' self-directed reading-writing-research processes. *Reading Research Quarterly, 31,* 122–135.

McCarthey, S.J. (1994). Authors, text, and talk: The internalization of dialogue from social interaction during writing. *Reading Research Quarterly, 29,* 200–231.

McCredie, D., Vukelich, C., & Roe, M. (1996, December). *Talk in the writing conference: A teacher's conversational strategies.* Presentation at the National Reading Conference, Charleston, SC.

McDaniel, E. (1987). Bibliography of text-analysis and writing-instruction software. *Journal of Advanced Composition, 7,* 139–169.

McGinley, W. (1992). The role of reading and writing while composing from sources. *Reading Research Quarterly, 27,* 226–248.

McGinley, W., & Kamberelis, G. (1996). Maniac Magee and Ragtime Tumpie: Children negotiating self and world through reading and writing. *Research in the Teaching of English, 30,* 75–113.

Montague, M., & Graves, A. (1993). Improving students' story writing. *Teaching Exceptional Children, 25,* 36–38.

Morocco, C. (1987). *Final report to US Office of Education.* Washington, DC: Special Education Programs, Educational Development Center.

Morocco, C., Dalton, B., & Tivnan, T. (1992). The impact of computer-supported writing instruction on 4th grade students with and without learning disabilities. *Reading and Writing Quarterly: Overcoming Learning Disabilities, 8,* 87–113.

Murray, D.M. (1985). *A writer teaches writing* (2nd ed.). Boston, MA: Houghton Mifflin.

Murray, D.M. (1990). *Shoptalk: Learning to write with writers.* Portsmouth, NH: Boynton/Cook.

Myers, M. (1985). *The teacher-researcher: How to study writing in the classroom.* Urbana, IL: ERIC Clearinghouse on Reading and Communication Skills and the National Council of Teachers of English.

Newkirk, T. (1987). The non-narrative writing of young children. *Research in the Teaching of English, 21,* 121–144.

Newkirk, T. (1994). The view from the mountains—A morning with Donald Graves. In T. Newkirk (Ed.), *Workshop 5: The writing process revisited.* Portsmouth, NH: Heinemann.

Newkirk, T. (1995). The writing conference as performance. *Research in the Teaching of English, 29,* 193–215.

Olson, M.W. (1990). The teacher as researcher: A historical perspective. In M.W. Olson (Ed.), *Opening the door to classroom research.* Newark, DE: International Reading Association.

O'Neil, J. (1996). On surfing—and steering—the net: Conversations with Crawford Kilian and Clifford Stoll. *Educational Leadership, 54,* 12–17.

Ong, W.J. (1982). *Orality and literacy: The technologizing of the world.* New York: Methuen.

Owston, P.D., Murphy, S., & Wideman, H.H. (1991). On and off computer writing of eighth grade students experienced in word processing. *Computers in the Schools, 8,* 67–87.

Owston, P.D., Murphy, S., & Wideman, H.H. (1992). The effects of word processing on students' writing quality and revision strategies. *Research in the Teaching of English, 26,* 249–276.

Paulsen, F., & Paulsen, P. (1994). *A guide for judging portfolios.* Portland, OR: Multnomah Education Service District.

Perl, S. (1979). The composing processes of unskilled college writers. *Research in the Teaching of English, 13,* 317–336.

Pianko, S. (1979). A description of the composing process of college freshman writers. *Research in the Teaching of English, 13,* 5–22.

Rhodes, L.K., & Shanklin, N. (1993). *Windows into literacy: Assessing learners K–8.* Portsmouth, NH: Heinemann.

Rief, L. (1993). *Seeking diversity.* Portsmouth, NH: Heinemann.

Rosenblatt, L. (1989). Writing and reading: The transactional theory. In J. Mason (Ed.), *Reading and writing connections* (pp. 153–176). Boston, MA: Allyn & Bacon.

Russell, R.G. (1991, April). *A meta-analysis of word processing and attitudes and the impact on the quality of writing*. Paper presented at the Annual Meeting of the American Educational Research Association, Chicago, IL.

Salinger, T., & Chittenden, E. (1994). Analysis of an early literacy portfolio: Consequences for instruction. *Language Arts, 71*, 446–451.

Sawkins, M.W. (1970). *The oral responses of selected fifth grade children to questions concerning their written expression*. Unpublished doctoral dissertation, State University of New York, Buffalo.

Scardamalia, M., & Bereiter, C. (1996). Engaging students in a knowledge society. *Educational Leadership, 54*, 6–11.

Schultz, K. (1994). "I want to be good; I just don't get it": A fourth grader's entrance into a literacy community. *Written Communication, 11*, 381–413.

Selfe, C. (1992). Preparing English teachers for the virtual age: The case for technology critics. In G.E. Hawisher & P. LeBlanc (Eds.), *Re-imagining computers and composition: Teaching and research in the virtual age*. Portsmouth, NH: Boynton/Cook.

Shanahan, T., & Lomax, R. (1986). An analysis and comparison of theoretical models of the reading-writing relationship. *Journal of Educational Psychology, 78*, 116–123.

Sipe, L. (1996). *The construction of literary understandings by first and second graders in response to picture storybook readalouds*. Unpublished doctoral dissertation, The Ohio State University, Columbus.

Smith, F. (1983). Reading like a writer. *Language Arts, 60*, 558–567.

Snider, M.A., Lima, S.S., & DeVito, P.J. (1994). Rhode Island's literacy portfolio assessment project. In S.W. Valencia, E.H. Heibert, & P.P. Afflerbach (Eds.), *Authentic reading assessment: Practices and possibilities* (pp. 71–88). Newark, DE: International Reading Association.

Spandel, V., & Stiggins, R.J. (1997). *Creating writers: Linking writing assessment and instruction* (2nd ed.). New York: Longman.

Sperling, D. (1993). What's worth an "A"? Setting standards together. *Educational Leadership, 50*, 73–75.

Sperling, M. (1993) *The social nature of written text: A research-based review and summary of conceptual issues in the teaching of writing* (Concept Paper No. 8). Urbana, IL: National Council of Teachers of English.

Spivey, N., & King, J. (1989). Readers as writers composing from sources. *Reading Research Quarterly, 24*, 7–26.

Stiggins, R. (1988). Revitalizing classroom assessment: The highest instructional priority. *Phi Delta Kappan, 69*, 363–368.

Storeyard, J., Simmons, R., Stumpf, M., & Pavloglou, E. (1993). Making computers work for students with special needs. *Teaching Exceptional Children, 26*, 22–24.

Tierney, R.J., Carter, M.A., & Desai, L.E. (1991). *Portfolio assessment in the reading-writing classroom.* Norwood, MA: Christopher-Gordon.

Tierney, R., Soter, A., O'Flahavan, J., & McGinley, W. (1989). The effects of reading and writing upon thinking critically. *Reading Research Quarterly, 24,* 134–169.

Tobin, L. (1994). Introduction: How the writing process was born—and other conversion narratives. In L. Tobin & T. Newkirk (Eds.), *Taking stock: The writing process movement in the '90s.* Portsmouth, NH: Boynton/Cook.

Treiman, R. (1993). *Beginning to spell.* New York: Oxford University Press.

Valencia, S.W., & Place, N.A. (1994). Literacy portfolios for teaching, learning, and accountability: The Bellevue literacy assessment project. In S.W. Valencia, E.H. Heibert, & P.P. Afflerbach (Eds.), *Authentic reading assessment: Practices and possibilities* (pp. 134–156). Newark, DE: International Reading Association.

Wilde, S. (1988). Learning to spell and punctuate: A study of eight- and nine-year-old children. *Language and Education: An International Journal, 2,* 35–59.

Wilde, S. (1992). *You kan red this!* Portsmouth, NH: Heinemann.

Winograd, K. (1993). Selected writing behaviors of fifth graders as they composed original mathematics story problems. *Research in the Teaching of English, 27,* 369–394.

Author Index

Page references followed by *f* indicate figures.

A

Abbott, R., 44
Abouzeid, M., 65
Adams, V.A., 127
Alexander, L., 16
Applebee, A.N., 71, 72, 73, 88
Ashton, T., 103
Atwell, N., 3, 31, 38
Au, K.H., 118
Avery, C., 3, 39, 81

B

Bagge-Rynerson, B., 83
Baker, E.L., 117
Bangert-Drowns, R.L., 97, 98
Baran, P., 90
Barham, I.H., 127
Bear, D., 65
Beers, J., 61
Bereiter, C., 6, 11, 12, 13, 24, 53,
    54, 55, 56, 91, 95
Boyle, C., 21, 122, 124, 126
Braddock, R., 2
Bratcher, S., 123
Britton, J., 7, 51
Bruce, B., 99
Burgess, T., 51
Burtis, P.J., 95

C

Calkins, L.M., 3, 29, 38, 59
Camp, R., 114
Carr, P.G., 12, 14
Carter, M.A., 111
Cazden, D., 66
Chapman, M., 55–56
Chittenden, E., 114
Cioffi, G., 25
Clark, M.H., 106
Clarke, L., 63
Cleary, B., 16
Cochran-Smith, M., 3, 96, 100
Cooper, C.R., 125, 126
Cooper, M., 10
Cordiero, P., 66
Cormier, R., 106
Countryman, J., 79

D

Dahl, K., 25
Daiute, C., 61, 101, 102
Dalton, B., 102
De Vito, P.J., 118
Desai, L.E., 111
Dickinson, D.K., 99
DiPardo, A., 44, 94
DiPardo, M., 94

Doctorow, E.L., 16
Dyson, A.H., 2, 5, 6, 8, 23, 26, 27, 28, 34, 43, 47, 53

E

Eckhoff, B., 81, 82
Elley, W.B., 127
Emig, J., 7

F

Farnan, N., 46
Fearn, L., 46
Finders, M., 45
Fitzgerald, J., 40–41, 58, 60
Fletcher, R., 3, 38
Flower, L.S., 8–9, 9*f*, 10
Forster, E.M., 16
Frank, L.A., 52
Fraser, J., 39
Freedman, S., 2, 5, 6, 7, 39, 44
Freppon, P., 25
Fry, D.J.W., 127
Fyfe, R., 74

G

Gates, B., 92
Gearhart, M., 117
Gentry, J., 61
Gere, A.R., 44
Giacobbe, M., 66
Gilbert, S.W., 136
Gill, J.T., 65
Gillet, J., 61
Goddin, M.A.P., 127
Goldstein, A.A., 12, 14
Gordon, C.J., 79
Graves, A., 103
Graves, D., 3, 23, 24, 37–38
Gunnarsson, B.L., 10

H–I

Haas, C., 94, 95, 101, 102
Hall, N., 67
Hallenbeck, M.J., 15
Hancock, M., 84
Hansen, J., 81
Harp, B., 111
Harper, K., 77, 78
Harwayne, S., 3, 38
Hawisher, G., 102
Hayes, J.R., 8–9, 9*f*, 10
Henderson, E., 61
Herman, J.L., 115, 116, 117
Hillocks, G., 2, 126, 127
Holzman, M., 10
Hudson, S., 43
Hughes, G., 121, 122
Invernizzi, M., 65

J

Jensen, J., 2
Johnson, N.L., 119, 120
Johnston, F., 65
Jones, I., 99

K

Kahn, J., 96, 100
Kamberelis, G., 29
Kellogg, S., 16
Kieley, C., 103
Kilian, C., 108
King, J., 74, 76, 77
Koretz, D., 116
Kroll, B., 53
Kucer, S., 86

L

Lamb, H., 127
Lane, B., 61
Langer, J., 30, 32, 52, 56, 71, 72, 73, 86, 88

LeBlanc, P., 93, 94
Lensmire, T., 44, 46
Lewis, G., 74
Lewis, R.B., 103, 107
Lima, S.S., 118
Lloyd, P., 16, 19
Lloyd-Jones, R., 2
Lomax, R., 86
Lyman, R.L., 2
Lytle, S., 3

M–N

MacGillivray, L., 26
MacInnis, D., 79
Many, J., 74
Markham, L.R., 60
Martin, N., 51
McCarthey, S.J., 40–42
McCredie, D., 42
McDaniel, E., 93
McGinley, W., 29, 86
McLeod, A., 51
Michaels, S., 99
Mitchell, E., 74
Montague, M., 103
Morocco, C., 102
Murphy, S., 100, 101, 102
Murray, D.M., 6, 15, 16
Myers, M., 3
Newkirk, T., 39, 56

O

O'Connor, F., 16
O'Flahavan, J., 86
Olson, M.W., 3
O'Neil, J., 108
Ong, W.J., 93
Owston, P.D., 100, 101, 102

P

Paris, C.L., 96, 100

Paulsen, F., 114
Paulsen, P., 114
Pavloglou, E., 103
Pellegrini, A.D., 99
Perl, S., 7, 17
Pianko, S., 7
Place, N.A., 118
Plato, 93

R

Rhodes, L.K., 111
Rief, L., 3, 39
Robinson, A., 67
Roe, M., 42
Rosen, H., 51
Rosenblatt, L., 82
Russell, R.G., 96

S

Salinger, T., 114
Sawkins, M.W., 20
Scardamalia, M., 6, 11, 12, 13, 24,
    53, 54, 55, 56, 91, 95
Schoer, L., 2
Schultz, K., 44
Selfe, C., 108
Shanahan, T., 86
Shanklin, N., 111
Simmons, R., 103
Sipe, L., 82, 85
Skolnick, D., 39
Smith, F., 81, 96, 100
Snider, M.A., 118
Soter, A., 86
Spandel, V., 111, 112, 113, 122, 123
Sperling, M., 2, 39, 121, 122, 124
Spivey, N., 74, 76, 77
Stamm, C., 40–41
Stiggins, R., 111, 112, 113, 121,
    122, 123
Stoll, C., 108
Storeyard, J., 103

152

Stumpf, M., 103
Sutcliff, R., 16

T

Templeton, S., 65
Tetroe, J., 95
Tierney, R.J., 86, 111
Tivnan, T., 102
Tobin, L., 47, 48
Treiman, R., 61, 62

V

Valencia, S.W., 118
Vukelich, C., 42

W

Watson-Gregeo, K., 99
Whittaker, A.K., 117
Wideman, H.H., 100, 101, 102
Wilde, S., 64, 65, 66
Winters, L., 115, 116
Wyllie, M., 127

Y

Yolan, J., 17

Subject Index

Page references followed by *f* indicate figures.

A

B

C

K

L

M

N–O

P–Q

PROBLEM SOLVING, 19, 33, 135
PRODUCT VERSUS PROCESS, 48
PUNCTUATION, 66–67, 70, 126–127, 132
PURPOSE OF WRITING, 7
QWERTY KEYBOARD, 104

R

REFLEXIVE WRITING, 7
RESEARCH. *See also specific topics*: assessment, 111–133; for fiction, 17; future possibilities, 19–21, 34–36, 49–50, 69–70, 88–89, 108–109, 130–133, 138–139; into practice, 3, 134. *See also* instruction; qualitative versus quantitative, 2–3; spelling, 62–65; technology and, 93–98
REVISION, 57–61, 68, 69; Calkins's research and, 59; procedural support for, 60–61
RHETORICAL PROBLEMS, 10
RHODE ISLAND LITERACY PORTFOLIO ASSESSMENT PROJECT, 118–119
RUBRICS, 122–125, 132

S

SCAFFOLDING, 43, 73
SELF, 34
SELF-INVOLVEMENT, 84
SELF-TALK, 77–78
SOCIAL FUNCTION, 10–11, 28, 35, 43–44, 56, 135
SOCIOLINGUISTICS, 10
SOFTWARE FOR WRITING, 95, 101, 103–104, 136–137
SOURCES, WRITING FROM, 74–77, 88; information use, 75–76; outcomes, 76–77
SPECIAL NEEDS STUDENTS. *See* learning disabled students
SPELLING, 61–66, 70; case studies, 64–65; comparative research, 62–64; invented, 62, 63; picture sorting, 65; resources, 65–66; transitional, 63; word hunting, 66; word recognition, 63; word sorting, 65
STRATEGIES FOR WRITING, 18–19, 30–31, 79–80; free association, 79–80; increasing problem difficulty, 80; question directed, 79
SYMBOLIC FORM, 28, 35

T

TASK ENVIRONMENT, 9*f*, 10, 135
TEACHER RESEARCHER ONLINE, 105
TEACHERS. *See also* instruction: as collaborators, 73; comments on papers, 127–128; complexity of tasks, 136; importance of research to, 2; as mod-